D1591027

Pete Gray

One-Armed Wonder

One-Armed Wonder

Pete Gray, Wartime Baseball,
and the American Dream

by WILLIAM C. KASHATUS

with a foreword by BILL BORST

McFarland & Company, Inc., Publishers
Jefferson, North Carolina, and London

Front cover: *Pete Gray completes a swing at the plate in the second game of a doubleheader (April 22, 1945), at Chicago against the White Sox (courtesy of Associated Press)*

Illustration on page i courtesy of Rebecca Smith

British Library Cataloguing-in-Publication data are available

Library of Congress Cataloguing-in-Publication Data

Kashatus, William C., 1959–
    One-armed wonder : Pete Gray, wartime baseball, and the American
dream / by William Kashatus; with a foreword by Bill Borst.
        p. cm.
    Includes bibliographical references and index.
    ISBN 0-7864-0094-3 (sewn softcover: 55# alk. paper) ∞
    1. Gray, Pete. 2. Baseball players—United States—Biography.
3. Baseball—United States—History. I. Title.
GV865.G66K37 1995
796.357′092—dc20
    [B]   95-5143
                                                        CIP

Manufactured in the United States of America

McFarland & Company, Inc., Publishers
  Box 611, Jefferson, North Carolina 28640

In memory of my surrogate grandfather,
John Dada Kashatus,
who shared his family, heritage, and
passionate love for baseball with me.
If they play the game in heaven,
I know he's pitching for the Glen Lyon Condors

Acknowledgments

WRITING A BOOK about a professional baseball player whose career ended a decade before I was born would have been impossible without the assistance of a number of people. At the top of the list are the family and friends of Pete Gray, as well as those he played with and against over the years of his remarkable career: John Andrezeyewski, John Barno, Tony Burgas, Avron Fogelman, Don Gutteridge, Al Hollingsworth, John, Michael and Stephen Howryshko, Mike Kreevich, Ed Perluke, Lou Pizont, Nelson Potter, Phil Rizzuto, Tex Shirley, Eddie Sincavage, Levy Sokowloski, Andrew Sweeney, Bertha Vedor, and William Wyshner.

The staff of the National Baseball Library at the Baseball Hall of Fame was extremely helpful. Among those to whom I am most indebted are Bill Deane, senior research associate; his associates, Paul Cunningham and Ken Fetterman; Patricia Kelly, the library's photo collection manager; and her assistant Bill Burdick. Special thanks are also due to Mary Ruth Kelly, executive director of the Wyoming Historical and

Geological Society; her associate, Wendy Franklin; Steve Gietschier, director of historical records at the *Sporting News*; Thomas J. Hickey, advertising director for *Sports Illustrated*; Patricia La Pointe, reference librarian at the Memphis Shelby County Public Library; Pam Nicholson and Jean McClellan of the Betteman Archives; Joe Canale and Jack Simon of Associated Press Wide World Photos; Ray Blockus and Carol Thomas of the *Wilkes-Barre Times Leader*; Ted Tornow, public relations director for the Memphis Chicks Baseball Club; Robert Little and Lorene Wolff of Allied Photocolor of St. Louis; Terrence Keenan, special collections librarian at Syracuse University Library; Robert Janasov of Luzerne County Community College; the Reverend Gerald J. Gurka and Mary Kempinski of St. Joseph's Roman Catholic Church, Wanamie, PA; Mary Gavarecki of Mar-Jo Photography; and Rebecca Smith of Temple University's Tyler School of Art.

Among those who deserve special mention are Bill Borst, the Baseball Professor, who generously agreed to write a foreword to this book; Bob Broeg who covered the Browns for the *St. Louis Post-Dispatch* during the war years; Harrington Crissey of the Society for American Baseball Research; David Jordan, whose work on *Hal Newhouser and the Burden of Wartime Ball* inspired me to write about Pete Gray; Dave Kindred of *The Sporting News*, and William Mead, who encouraged the publication of this book despite all of the obstacles to be overcome.

Special thanks are also due to the administration, faculty, staff, and student body of the William Penn Charter School for being so supportive of my desire for professional growth as a writer. I am also grateful to Peter Baumann, Alex Carver, Kevin Free; Jeremy, Jonathan, and Tommy John Kashatus, Mike McCabe, and Ed Molush for their moral support and friendship over the years of this enterprise; and to Pete Gray, Tim McCarver, and Mike Schmidt, for renewing my love of the game and my faith in its heroes.

Above all, I am indebted to my family—Jackie, Tim, Ann, Jack, Billy, Mom and Dad. Their steadfast encouragement and unconditional love have made me the biggest winner of all. For that, I will always be grateful.

Table of Contents

Foreword
(Bill Borst)

A S THE FOUNDER of the St. Louis Browns Historical Society, an organization which has dedicated itself to the re-establishment and the maintenance of the team's historical legacy, I have had the good fortune of meeting and enjoying warm friendships with the likes of Roy Sievers, "Footsie" Lenhardt, Babe Martin, Bill Jennings, Ed Mickelson, Hank Arft, Ned Garver, and many other familiar and maybe not so familiar names of the past. I often marvel at their dignified demeanor and the obvious contrast to some of the players of today, who are more haughty, distant and sometimes just unfriendly. These men were definitely men for all seasons, not just idealized boys of summer.

Nevertheless, when the name *Browns* is mentioned, there are usually a few predictable reactions. Many people confuse our beloved team with Cleveland's football franchise. Some refer to the Brownies as that "other team in St. Louis," the one that played in the shadow of the National

League Cardinals. Others seem only to remember Eddie Gaedel, the 3' 7" pinch hitter who walked on cue and, after reaching first base, trotted off the field and into the history books forever. And of course, there are still others who remark, "Those guys were so bad that they actually used a one-armed player."

Although I get a bit testy when I hear these remarks, I restrain myself and simply remind the critic that the Browns fielded some great teams prior to 1926 and emerged again in 1944 to capture a pennant. Of course, the true baseball cynics will always retort: "That '44 team competed during the war years when the game was so bad that *even the Browns* could win a pennant." As if they all were not playing on the same size diamond and the balls were of a different size and weight!

Amidst all the popular misconceptions and folklore surrounding the wartime Browns is the figure of Pete Gray, the one-armed wonder who platooned in the outfield during the '45 season. Gray may not have been a great player—not a George Sisler or even a Vern Stephens—but he could play the game. In fact, he was one of only 20,000 men to play in a major league game. Many members of the Browns Historical Society remember him as the "major leaguer who did with one arm what most could not do with two." That was true back then and it is still true today. It is about time his life made it into print.

William Kashatus has filled an obvious void with his biography of the former Brownie. He has done it with compassion, concern, and an innate respect and admiration for someone who did something heroic at home while others died abroad. He has revived the distant memory of a man who carried his cross in life with courage, determination and a relentless fire in his gut that has only been rivaled in the history of major league baseball by that of Ty Cobb, Jackie Robinson, and Pete Rose.

In an era that stresses collectivism, dependency and victimization, Pete Gray stands as a sterling example of rugged individualism. He is a Hemingwayesque character, whose grace under pressure served as an inspiration to anyone who ever felt the odds of life were against him. Pete Gray never looked for charity, nor did he sit and feel sorry for long. He could have been the inspiration for the recruiting slogan the U.S. Army employs: *Be the Best You Can Be.* Gray always knew that and now, thanks to Kashatus, the reader knows it too.

St. Louis, Missouri, March 1, 1994

Introduction

WHEN I WAS a young boy my father introduced me to Pete Gray, the one-armed baseball player who captured the attention of the sports world in 1945 when he played outfield for the St. Louis Browns. Gray, who was in his mid-fifties at the time, impressed me as a kind-hearted, gentle human being who took a genuine interest in young people.

I sat and watched in awe as he demonstrated how, in one swift motion, he could catch a baseball, remove it from his glove, and throw. All of this with just one arm! Before we parted ways, Gray patted me on the head and handed me an autographed baseball, saying: "Remember me when you make it to the big leagues."

Pete Gray was a boy's hero, what I came to expect of every professional baseball player. What I didn't know—and would not realize until I grew older—was that while Gray was a hero to many, he had been manipulated by club owners as well as by the media, maligned by many of his teammates, and left to wonder just how good a ballplayer he really was.

Most baseball historians credit Pete Gray's professional career to the lack of quality players in the major leagues during World War II. Some claimed that the Browns purchased Gray as a gate attraction, while others viewed the one-armed outfielder as a "curiosity item" or public relations ploy to divert the attention of a war-weary nation.[1] More disturbing is the fact that Pete Gray did not enjoy the wholehearted respect of his team-mates, many of whom believed that his presence in the lineup cost the 1945 Browns the chance to repeat as American League champions. There were even those Browns players who regarded Gray as an ill-tempered rookie with a chip on his shoulder who knew he didn't belong in the big leagues. But I remembered a much different Pete Gray than either the baseball historians or the '45 Browns, and I set out to write about him.

Twenty years had passed since my father had introduced me to Pete Gray. Over that time he had become something of a personal folk hero. Born as Pete Wyshner, he was raised in the same small northeastern Pennsylvania coal town as my grandparents. Like many of the towns-people, his parents were Lithuanian immigrants who came to this country in search of the American Dream. While they tried to realize that dream in the anthracite coal mines of the Wyoming Valley, they taught their children that hard work was the only true measure of a person's worth. Pete Wyshner learned that lesson well.

As a young man, he chased after his boyhood dream to play major league baseball, and, despite the loss of his right arm, he caught up with that dream and saw it come true. For me, a thirty-year-old baseball romantic trying to recapture a moment of his youth, Gray represented the underdog who dared to succeed in spite of his less-than-humble beginnings. Unlike so many others who came from similar circum-stances, chased their dreams, and failed to realize them, Pete Gray had beaten the odds and won. These were the feelings that motivated me as I mustered the courage to introduce myself, once again, to the one-armed ball player who had asked me to remember him two decades earlier. What I found astonished me.

Gray's appearance had changed remarkably little from my boyhood memory of him, but this time he appeared to be more introverted and highly sensitive about his missing arm. When I mentioned my interest in writing about his season with the Browns, he replied, "There's not much to tell." He was on guard this time, as he was with most adult strangers. Although the memory of my childhood visit with him elicited a smile, my questions met with terse responses, and after five minutes I felt as if I was intruding.

"One last thing, Pete," I said, determined to satisfy my own curiosity, "how would you like to be remembered?" The question cut him to the quick. He wasn't prepared for it and he hesitated.

"Let me tell you something," he finally snapped. "I spent my entire youth working to make it to the big leagues. When I first got there it was great. But since that time it's all been downhill."

The response was sharp and caustic. I couldn't believe that this was the same person I had grown to admire. I tried to hide my disappointment by quickly retorting, "You sound very bitter."

"Bitter?" he said. And with a smile, he added, "Nah, I'm just joking with you!" I couldn't tell if he was being sarcastic or if this was his way to dismiss me and the subject once and for all.

"Look," he said, wanting to end the conversation. "You go and write whatever the hell you want to write. Just leave me alone." And with that Pete Gray went on his way.

There was a part of me that wanted to forget about Gray, to dismiss him as a cantankerous old man just as the baseball writers had done. But my curiosity told me that there was much more to him than even he wanted to admit himself. And so, I kept returning to his hometown of Nanticoke to talk with his friends and, on occasion, with Pete Gray himself. He began to trust me a bit more when he saw that I was genuinely interested in his friends and in his current life. I tried to fill the missing gaps by writing to the newspapers in all the cities and small towns where he played semi-professional and minor league baseball, collecting box scores and articles that would give me some kind of insight into his personality. I corresponded with those of his teammates from the old St. Louis Browns who were still alive and tried to square their nostalgic memories of Gray with the reality of the quotations they had given to *The Sporting News* in 1945. If nothing else, I became the world's greatest collector of Pete Gray photographs and newspaper articles. And maybe, in the process, even a friend to my boyhood hero.

In the end I discovered that all Pete Gray really wanted from the baseball writers, as well as his teammates, was respect for his integrity as a professional baseball player. He wanted to be judged by his ability, not to be exploited for his handicap. And yet, 50 years after completing his major league career, Gray still wonders whether he had proved himself as a professional athlete. When I pointed out that he had compiled a .333 batting average, stole 68 bases and won the Southern Association's Most Valuable Player Award in 1944 when he played for the Memphis Chicks, it did not seem to convince my aging hero that those minor league achievements made up for the .218 average he posted with the Browns in his only major league season. But the significance of Gray's career cannot be measured by the statistics he compiled; rather it is to be found in the example he set for others.

To be sure, America's involvement in World War II did help to make Pete Gray a professional baseball player. Most professional athletes will admit, if they are honest, that a certain degree of luck and circumstance favored them in their climb to the top. But once Gray arrived at the top, he did more than his fair share for baseball and for the nation.

For wounded veterans and their families, the one-armed outfielder was a heroic symbol on the home front. Gray asked for no sympathy from anyone; rather, he stepped up to the plate, holding his bat in his left hand—a picture of defiance—and he competed on even terms with all rivals. Gray's example gave these veterans hope that they, too, could succeed in whatever career they chose as long as they gave it their all.

He delivered this message on playing fields across the country, as well as in veterans' hospitals where he spoke with amputees, reassuring them that there was hope in their future. And yet, when he was praised for his courage on the ballfield, Gray with characteristic humility, remarked: "There is no courage about me. Courage belongs on the battlefield, not on the baseball diamond. But if I can prove to any boy who has been physically handicapped that he, too, can compete with the best—well, then, I've done my little bit."

World War II might have helped to make Pete Gray a major league baseball player, but there is no question that it made him an American hero. Although I never had the opportunity to watch him perform on a ball diamond, Gray can play on my field of dreams any day, because he started out in life at a disadvantage and still managed to collect his 51 hits in the major leagues. Few men have that kind of determination to succeed in life; fewer still have the capacity to make a difference in the lives of so many others. *Nothing*—not even the baseball historians—can ever take those achievements away from Pete Gray.

WILLIAM C. KASHATUS
Philadelphia, Pennsylvania
Spring 1994

Pennsylvania's Wyoming Valley

"Forty years I worked with pick and drill
Down in the mines against my will,
The Coal King's slave, but now it's passed;
Thanks be to God I am free at last."

—*From the tombstone of an anthracite miner*

L ONG BEFORE COAL was king in northeastern Pennsylvania, the beautiful valley was made up of rolling hills, fertile meadowlands, and thick forests abundant with wildlife. Tucked away between the mountain ranges west of the Poconos, this small, tranquil haven was known only to its original Indian inhabitants and the Moravian missionaries who navigated the Susquehanna River searching for converts to their Christian faith. Over the course of the eighteenth century, however, the Wyoming Valley became the scene of a bitter struggle

7

among Connecticut Yankees, Pennsylvania settlers, and the Delaware
and Iroquois nations, all of whom claimed title to the land. Their dispute
erupted into a prolonged civil conflict known as the Pennamite wars and,
later, during the Revolutionary era, into a bloody Indian massacre of
white settlers.[1]

But it was another struggle, one that occurred at the turn of the nineteenth century, that would alter its geographical and demographic land-
scape forever. It was a conflict between immigrants. It pitted the older,
more established settlers from northern and western Europe against the
newly-arrived immigrants from southern and eastern Europe. More
specifically, it was a struggle for dominion over an anthracite culture.
While the "old immigrants"—primarily English and Welsh in origin—
were skilled laborers, foremen, and colliery owners who settled in the
Wyoming Valley during the early nineteenth century and established the
coal industry, the "new immigrants" were largely unskilled workers who
arrived from Lithuania, Russia, Italy, and Poland after the American
Civil War. They had been drawn by the lure of the American Dream and
a burgeoning anthracite industry which they hoped would serve as their
ticket to success. Increasingly, these Eastern Europeans became the
backbone of labor in the Wyoming Valley.

The differences between these two groups were cultural, but they
often manifested themselves in the living conditions, working relation-
ships, patterns of mobility, and physical violence that characterized the
life of the Valley's anthracite culture.[2] By the 1940s, the grandchildren
of these Eastern European immigrants had triumphed; they had become
the skilled laborers, the union leaders, and, in some cases, the coal
operaters themselves. They had achieved the American Dream, but it
came at a price.

The anthracite industry violated a once beautiful valley, leaving
mountainous black banks of coal refuse, waste piles of slate and rock,
and only scrawny little birch trees to dominate a region once rich in
woodland evergreens, oaks, and pines. It polluted the sparkling streams
and creeks, turning many of them black with coal dust and redolent with
the stench of sulphur. Even the Susquehanna River, which once weaved
its way through the Valley like a silver thread, bears a permanent dark
tinge, a reminder that the river basin collapsed in the 1950s, flooding out
the empty coal beds and destroying whatever anthracite mining might
have still existed. But the mountains still remain. The mountains continue
to serve as a protective barrier against the outside world and a fear of the

unknown beyond. Not only do they afford the Valley's inhabitants a sense of security, a sense of belonging, and a sense of home, but they preserve a mentality which is distinctively "immigrant" in nature. Perhaps that is why the Wyoming Valley never really changes.

The refreshing innocence of the Valley's people is not much different than that of their Eastern European ancestors who arrived at the turn of the nineteenth century. Some would call it a "provincial" attitude but that would be much too simple. It is rather an ambivalent outlook which encourages ambition and personal enterprise but never at the expense of community solidarity. It respects individual achievement as long as the individual remembers "where he came from" and returns often enough to acknowledge his past. It is an outlook held by a very passionate people who, if they "like" somebody, they "like 'em hard." But God help the person they don't like! And yet for all of their ambivalence, the people of Pennsylvania's Wyoming Valley are essentially very genuine human beings. They have always been hard workers, the backbone of labor in the United States. Those who become extremely successful embrace a work ethic grounded in an almost pathologic fear of failure. Like their coal mining forefathers, they still believe that self-respect, a good education, and plain, honest hard work will enable the individual to rise above his humble circumstances and become a "somebody." Most of all, they care about themselves and about each other. That is why they inherited the title "Valley with a Heart" during the Great Depression of the 1930s.

To understand the culture of the Wyoming Valley, then, is to understand the mountains that surround it and to appreciate the sense of shelter, security, and belonging they have always afforded the people who live in the valley below. It is also the only way to understand the immigrant mentality that inspired Pete Gray to beat the odds and go beyond those mountains in search of his dream to become a major league baseball player. His story begins with the emigration of his parents from their native Lithuania to the United States in the 1890s.

Antoinette and Peter Wyshner were peasant farmers who lived in the countryside surrounding the town of Vilna. Like most Lithuanians, the Wyshners had experienced the persecution of an oppressive Russian government.[3] Under the reign of Tsar Alexander Romanov II, Russia sought to forcibly assimilate all neighboring ethnic groups into its own culture. The initial suppression of the Lithuanian press and government was followed by sporadic pogroms aimed at the destruction of the Catholic church in favor of establishing Russian Orthodoxy as the national religion of Lithuania. Catholic resistance only resulted in more severe raids by the Cossack armies and, ultimately, in a stringent land policy which encouraged Russian colonization in the duchy. Individual holdings were confiscated and redistributed at prices affordable only to the Russian gentry, leaving the small peasant farmer with less productive land, if any at all. Even these meager holdings were mortgaged in the 1870s when economic depression forced many peasants to borrow money. Interest payments became so high that many had to sell their few personal possessions and become hired laborers. With the introduction of compulsory service in the Russian army in the 1890s, the Russification process had became insufferable for a once proud and independent people.[4]

This forced assimilation and its demeaning effects drove the Wyshners from their native Lithuania for the promise of a better future in America. After an unsuccessful attempt at establishing a new home in Chicago, the Wyshners relocated in Pennsylvania's Wyoming Valley. Attracted by the prospect of steady work in the coal mines, Peter Wyshner hoped to find a good job, work hard at it, and save enough money to buy a house and raise a family. His decision to resettle in northeastern Pennsylvania would eventually provide all of those things.[5]

Northeastern Pennsylvania's anthracite region, bounded on the west by the branches of the Susquehanna River, on the east by the Lehigh River, and to the south by the Blue Mountains, once contained three-quarters of the earth's anthracite coal deposits. It provided the entire East Coast with the fuel it needed for consumer heating and industrial production. The area was divided into four coal fields: the Southern field, located primarily in Schuykill County; the Western Middle field which cut across Northumberland, Columbia, and Schuykill counties; the Eastern Middle field, at the southern end of Luzerne County; and the Northern field which extended from Susquehanna County in the north to Luzerne County in the south.[6] In 1880 these four coalfields produced 27,974,532 tons of coal with a total workforce of 73,373 men. Three decades later, annual production had nearly tripled to 83,683,994 tons, and the total workforce was 168,175 men. By 1917, the peak year of production, the four anthracite fields turned out 100,445,299 tons of coal, with a total workforce of 156,148 men.[7] Of all the fields, however, the most prodigious production of coal occurred in the Northern field.

At 6 miles in width and 55 miles in length, the Northern field was the largest and most productive coalfield of the anthracite region. It was

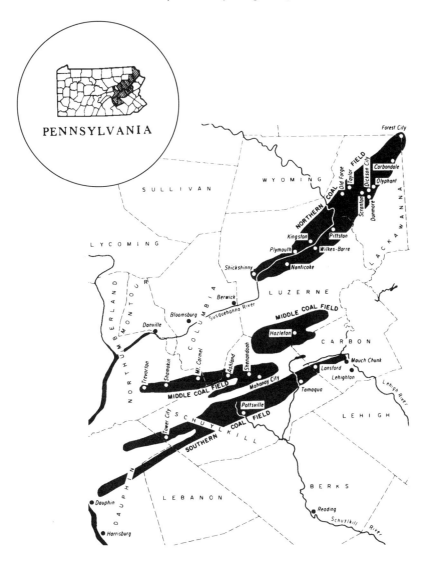

ANTHRACITE FIELDS

OF

PENNSYLVANIA

also the lifeblood of the Wyoming Valley. From 1910 to 1917, the Northern field produced nearly 35 million tons of coal annually.[8] This tremendous success was due to two major advantages it had over its neighboring fields to the south. First, operators found it easier to extract coal from the Northern field because the beds gradually dipped into the ground beginning at Forest City, reached a maximum depth at Wilkes-Barre, and outcropped again at the western end of the field around Nanticoke and Shickshinny. This horizontal pattern contained 20 coal-beds that were more accessible to miners than the deeper beds in the fields to the south. Second, the coal that was mined out of the Northern field was more marketable because it contained more carbon, making it much more pure. These two advantages made the Northern field a virtual treasure chest of the "black diamond."[9]

The Wyoming Valley, in particular, enjoyed major coal operations at Pittston, Wilkes-Barre, Plymouth, Glen Lyon, and Nanticoke. These were controlled by one of four companies: the Alden Coal Company; the Delaware, Lehigh, and Western Railroad (DL & W); the Lehigh & Wilkes-Barre Coal Company; and the Susquehanna Coal Company. Of these four coal companies, the DL & W was the largest, dominating both the mining and transportation of anthracite coal in the region. Established in the 1860s, the DL & W had acquired over 25,000 acres of land and built a railroad network that extended throughout Pennsylvania, New Jersey and New York. By 1900, the company was producing approximately 8 million tons of coal per year, employed about 15,000 workers and had accumulated assets totalling $50 million. Its production and wealth was second only to the Philadelphia and Reading Coal and Iron Company whose operations were primarily in the Middle and Southern coal fields.

DL & W's chief operations were located in the Nanticoke area and included the Auchincloss, Bliss, Loomis, and Truesdale collieries, each of which was considered an innovation at the time of its construction. Bliss, for example, was the oldest of the four collieries and the second largest producer of coal in the anthracite region by the early twentieth century. Auchincloss, built in 1901, soon eclipsed Bliss, producing nearly 145,000 tons of coal per year. It was also the deepest mine in the anthracite region at 2,000 feet, as well as the first electrically-driven coal breaker that processed anthracite by separating it from rock and slate. In 1905, DL & W improved its operations once again by opening the Truesdale Colliery in the Hanover section of Nanticoke.[10]

Truesdale Breaker, Hanover Section of Nanticoke, Pennsylvania, was the largest single coal-producing colliery in the Wyoming Valley. (Courtesy of the Wyoming Historical & Geological Society, Wilkes-Barre, Pennsylvania.)

Not only did Truesdale have the largest breaker in the world, but it was also the highest single coal-producing colliery and greatest employer in the Wyoming Valley. By 1913, Truesdale was producing over one million tons of coal per year and employed 1,739 men. A decade later, it was producing nearly five million tons of coal—20 percent of all the coal that was produced in the Wyoming Valley—and employing 2,108 men, most of whom were Lithuanian, Polish, or Russian immigrants.[11] DL & W's final innovation came in 1917 with the construction of the Loomis colliery. This operation was equal in size to Truesdale, but it was built of concrete, steel, and glass, a significant departure from the earlier wood structures that had dominated the anthracite industry. Shortly after, the DL & W was forced to divest itself of its coal properties by a federal law outlawing its monopoly on producing and transporting the coal. Although the corporation remained a major force in the transportation of coal in northeastern Pennsylvania, the Glen Alden Coal company assumed control of all DL & W coal properties in 1921.[12]

When Antoinette and Peter Wyshner arrived in the Wyoming Valley in 1911, DL & W was the largest employer in the area. The Wyshners settled in the Hanover section of Nanticoke where Peter found employment as a laborer at the Truesdale colliery. Since he was unskilled at coal mining, he had to work for a Welsh miner, learn the trade, and then apply to the state board of labor for a certificate.[13] He realized that the "streets weren't paved with gold" and that he would have to prove himself to his employers.

Like virtually all new immigrants when they first settled in the Wyoming Valley, Peter Wyshner was an obedient, loyal worker who, at first, simply sought to "survive" in this new society. His personal disposition reinforced the subservient attitude of the new immigrant. He was a shy man with a lot of patience. He did not stir up trouble with the more established Welsh and English miners nor did he ever challenge his role as a laborer—the lowest position in the anthracite hierarchy. Instead he fully intended to pay his dues knowing that some day his time would come. He *would* have his own house, his own family, and his own laborer. Antoinette, on the other hand, was not as patient.

She was an ambitious woman who wanted to acquire as much of the American Dream as soon as she possibly could. She goaded her husband to work harder, to ask for double shifts in the mines if necessary, so they could purchase a house of their own. When he failed to meet her demands, Antoinette allowed her aggressive nature to get the best of her. She disguised herself as a man and went to work at the Truesdale colliery for nearly a week until her ploy was discovered by a foreman.[14] Antoinette Wyshner wanted the finest of things in life. After all, that was why she immigrated to America, and now that she had arrived there was no reason, in her mind, why she shouldn't be able to enjoy all the benefits of American citizenship. Accordingly, she made it her business to account for every dime that was spent. To be certain, the streets of Hanover weren't paved with gold but this Lithuanian immigrant felt she deserved the best and she wouldn't settle for anything less.

Hanover, located at the eastern end of Nanticoke, was a small coal mining village of no more than 2,000 people when the Wyshners settled there in 1911. The town was a patchwork of self-contained ethnic communities whose members clung together for security and mutual support and held fast to their own languages and customs. Inevitably, community values and behavior became intimately shaped by the coal industry and dependent upon its prosperity and continued existence.

Almost every employable male worked for the DL & W either on the east end of town at the Truesdale operation or the west end of town at the Bliss colliery.

Thus, the Lithuanians, Ukrainians, Russians, Italians, and Poles who settled in Hanover largely conformed to the patterns of the coal industry, forging a society that not only adapted to the employment opportunities offered by the DL & W, but to the economic and cultural difficulties which characterized the coal industry itself: long hours, low wages, hazardous working conditions, and ethnic prejudice between the old and new immigrants.

Because of these adversities, the new immigrants built a strong network of kinship and communal relations which sustained its members by assisting in employment searches, social activities, and emotional support in periods of mourning. This community solidarity was reinforced by the church.

For Lithuanians in particular, the Catholic church offered a measure of security in their new American society. It was the one institution that they brought with them from the old world and one on which they lavished great wealth and affection. The priest, who was the most highly regarded authority figure in the town, served as the common man's guide to the mysterious spiritual world. Because he was called to serve God, being the only human who could communicate directly with the Divine, the priest was able to explain God's will and how it applied to the personal circumstances of his parishioners. Not surprisingly, many Eastern European immigrants volunteered their sons as altar boys in the hope that they too would be called to serve God and "do their family proud."[15]

There were four churches in Hanover: St. John's Ukrainian Church, St. Joseph's Lithuanian Catholic Church, the Russian Orthodox church, and a small Episcopal church. Each one served the spiritual needs of a particular ethnic group. For example, the few Welsh and English that lived in Hanover attended the Episcopal church, while the Russians and Ukrainians supported their own Orthodox churches. St. Joseph's primarily served the town's Lithuanian Catholics since the smaller contingents of Hanover's Polish and Italian Catholics preferred to attend mass in larger churches of their own ethnicity outside of the town. Despite the segregationist nature of these churches, they actually did serve as important vehicles for the new immigrants in the assimilation process.[16]

St. Joseph's Lithuanian Catholic Church (ca. 1926) was not only a place of wor-ship for the Wyshners and the other Lithuanian residents of Hanover, but also the center of their social life. In the 1920s, St. Joseph's established a baseball team known as the "Lithuanian Knights." Pete Gray would star for this team in the '30s when it was known as the Hanover Lits. (Courtesy of St. Mary's Roman Catholic Church, Hanover section of Nanticoke, Pennsylvania.)

At St. Joseph's Lithuanian Catholic Church, where the Wyshners attended mass, the parishioners often congregated to discuss and make sense of the political and social events of the day. It was more than a diversion from the daily routine of a coal miner's existence. It was often the only place to socialize with others. Their attendance at church functions was not limited to Sunday morning, simply because church functions were, in great measure, *social* functions which took place throughout the week. The Wyshners, like all of their Lithuanian neighbors, lavished great love and attention on St. Joseph's. Antoinette invested a great deal of her time cooking for church picnics in the summer and for chicken dinners in the winter. Peter often volunteered to do carpentry work or routine maintenance at the church or to construct the booths for the annual bazaar.[17] Regardless of the season, the Wyshners, like all new immigrants, put their backs to the wheel for their church. In return, the church introduced them to American traditions and customs. Chief among these traditions was baseball.

Throughout northeastern Pennsylvania, baseball flourished as a church-sponsored form of recreation and entertainment for coal miners and their families. As the sport was embraced by the children of immigrants, it became an important step in the assimilation process, providing a common meeting ground for the various social, ethnic, and religious groups in the anthracite region. Nearly every town had an amateur team and some as many as three or four. A few of these clubs would eventually become semiprofessional organizations whose best players tried out for the big leagues. A significant number succeeded too. Between 1876 and 1960, more than one hundred men from the anthracite region played, managed, or coached in the majors. Among the most outstanding were Hall of Famers Stan Coveleskie, Hughie Jennings, and Busky Harris.[18]

Coveleskie, who was born and raised in Shamokin, was the youngest of five ballplaying sons raised by Polish immigrants. A control pitcher, he averaged only one walk every 3.86 innings over a fourteen-year career with the Philadelphia Athletics, Cleveland Indians, Washington Senators and New York Yankees. His best years were with Cleveland, particularly the championship season of 1920 when he won three games against Brooklyn in the World Series. In those three games, Coveleskie allowed a total of two runs and two walks, struck out eight, and had an ERA of 0.67.

Hughie Jennings was the son of an immigrant coal miner. A red-headed, freckled-faced firebrand, he rose from his humble origins as a breaker boy to become one of baseball's most colorful characters. Jennings left his native Pittston in the 1890s to begin his professional career with the Baltimore Orioles. During his five seasons as the Orioles' shortstop, he never batted below .328. After playing for Brooklyn and Philadelphia, Jennings became the manager of the Detroit Tigers, leading them to three consecutive pennants.

Harris, like Jennings, hailed from Pittston. After leaving school at the age of 13, Harris worked at a local colliery until he got his break in pro ball with the Washington Senators in 1919. An exceptional fielder, he led American League second basemen in putouts four times and in double plays a record five consecutive times. In 1924 Harris became the player-manager for the Senators and led them to the only World Championship in club history. At age 27, he was also the youngest man ever to lead a team to the championship.[19]

Other outstanding players included Eddie Murphy, a native of White Mills who was an honest member of the infamous 1919 Chicago "Black Sox" teams accused of throwing the World Series; Mike Gazella of Olyphant, who played for the 1927 New York Yankees; Steve O'Neill of Minooka, one of four brothers in the majors and the manager of the 1945 World Champion Detroit Tigers; Mickey Witek of Luzerne, an outstanding second baseman for the New York Giants and Buck Freeman, a southpaw who pitched for Boston until they discovered his hitting abilities.[20] Converted into an outfielder, Freeman led the American League in 1903 with 13 home runs, 104 RBIs and 281 total bases, an impressive compilation during the "dead ball" era. His three triples in the World Series that year helped Boston defeat the Pittsburgh Pirates for the World Championship.[21] The Nanticoke area, in particular, produced some fine talent, including Dodger pitcher Bob Duliba, Steve Bilko and John Grodzicki of the St. Louis Cardinals, Harold Thompson of the Philadelphia Athletics, and Al Cihocki and Stan Pawloski of the Cleveland Indians. And, of course, Pete Gray of the St. Louis Browns.

For these Pennsylvanians, many the sons of coal miners, major league baseball was considered an escape from the difficult times and uncertain futures experienced by their fathers. A professional baseball career meant freedom from the most dangerous kind of employment, ethnic discrimination, and fluctuating wages. It also provided the new immigrant with a vehicle through which he could identify his American citizenship.

Baseball was a symbolic representation of the heart and mind of the American national character because it promised each individual the opportunity to step up to the plate and get his chance for glory. Regardless of his religious or ethnic background, the baseball player competed on even terms with his opponents and, in the process, crystallized the "rags-to-riches" success story that became so cherished among the first generation of Eastern European immigrants. The younger generations, on the other hand, were more secure in their American identity. They chose to attend or play the game because it was *their* pastime. They had grown up with it in school, on the streets, and in the newspapers. It was a rite of passage for them, as much a ritual as getting one's first job or the first taste of beer—symbols of the passage to adulthood. Unfortunately, even baseball could not always overcome the prejudice the new immigrants felt towards the Welsh and English miners, foremen, and coal operators who served as the major obstacle in their quest for the American Dream.

Hanover was owned by those Welsh and English immigrants. It was established in the 1880s as a coal mining village for cheap, new immigrant labor. While Lithuanians, Poles, Russians, Ukrainians, and Italians lived in the wood shanties and, later, double-block framed houses that comprised the town itself, the Welsh and English lived on the outskirts of the town. DL & W's coal operators lived in the Victorian mansions that lined the main street of Nanticoke proper, while the mine bosses and foremen also enjoyed commodious living quarters in the central or western end of Nanticoke. In 1911, the DL & W rewarded its most prized Welsh and English employees with a company housing project known as Concrete City. This was located just south of the Truesdale breaker but still far enough from the town of Hanover to preserve the ethnic segregation.[22]

Unlike the wood-frame company houses built before 1890, the Concrete City homes afforded their residents a great deal more luxury and privacy. The older shanties were rarely painted or plastered and seldom did they have more than two or three rooms. The kitchen was a multipurpose room where bathing, sleeping, and socializing took place as well as the daily cooking and eating. Concrete City, on the other hand, represented the wave of the future and afforded its favored residents a middle class lifestyle. Twenty double-block houses, enough to accommodate forty families, comprised the community. The houses were made of concrete, painted with dark green trim, and arranged in a rectangular fashion facing an enclosed courtyard. Each house had seven rooms: a

Concrete City was a company housing project constructed by the Delaware, Lehigh, and Western Railroad to reward its most prized Welsh and English mine employees. The project consisted of twenty double-block houses each one offering its residents a middle class lifestyle. (Courtesy of George Arents Research Library, Syracuse University.)

living room and dining room on the first floor, four bedrooms on the second; a pantry, and a cellar. Trees and shrubbery were planted outside and flower boxes attached beneath the front windows of each house. Four-foot sidewalks dotted with lamp posts separated the houses from the street and extended into the courtyard. By the summer of 1914, the DL & W had also provided a concrete swimming pool, a playground, and a baseball diamond for the children of the residents.

The DL & W stipulated that these homes were to be rented only to English-speaking workers, a policy meant to exclude the new Eastern European immigrants and favor the English and Welsh employees. Homes were specifically designated for the use of specialists — carpenters, foremen of high-producing coal veins, technicians, and blacksmiths. These employees were considered essential to Truesdale's record coal production and viewed as vital for the DL & W's profitable output. By keeping them happy, the ownership ensured the continuation of its success. It was a success, however, that was also founded on the exploitation of the Eastern European immigrant.[23]

Breaker Boys at work inside the Truesdale Colliery, ca. 1920. For 25¢ per day these boys, not much older than eight years of age, would remove the slate, rock and wood from the anthracite that had been siphoned into various sizes at the top of the breaker. (Courtesy of Mar-Jo's Photography Studio, Glen Lyon, PA.)

The DL & W was the largest of the coal companies and the major employer in the Nanticoke area. It owned everything in Hanover— homes, stores, taverns, and even the people themselves. Company profits were secured, in large part, because of the poor wages they paid their unskilled workers. In the absence of child labor laws, a young male could go to work as a breaker boy as early as the age of eight years. For 25¢ per day he would sit on the ground floor of the breaker next to a coal chute and remove the slate, rock, and wood from the anthracite that had been siphoned into various sizes at the top of the breaker. By the age of ten, many of these boys had permanently lost their fingernails, and it was not uncommon to find hunchbacks among them. Their fathers, most of whom were unskilled Lithuanian and Polish laborers working under the direction of a state-certified Welsh or English coal miner, earned anywhere from 75¢ to $1.25 per day, depending upon the number of coal cars he filled and the generosity of his boss.[24] The poor pay was only surpassed by the hazardous working conditions to which these immigrants were exposed.

Cave-ins were common, especially if wooden supports were improperly positioned when a coal vein was mined out. Flooding was also common because the mining was done hundreds of feet below the Susquehanna River bed. Runaway mine cars and unpredictable explosions were daily concerns for these immigrants. In fact, from 1890 to 1910, there were over 5,000 deaths in the Wyoming Valley that occurred as a result of these types of mining accidents. In 1904 alone, 595 men died in the Valley's mines; the worst accident being an explosion that occurred at Auchincloss, claiming the lives of nearly 100 men.[25] Essentially, a coal miner faced the very real threat of death on a daily basis. Even if he was fortunate enough to escape these immediate dangers, he would eventually be forced to contend with "black lung," a respiratory disease caused by years of inhaling coal dust. The majority of these men would end up coughing themselves to death for less than subsistence wages.

Even the simple pleasures of life were controlled by the English and Welsh. They were the people who owned and operated the company stores, shops, and saloons that lined the business district of Hanover's Front Street. Purchases would be deducted from the laborer's weekly salary, and there was no such thing as credit. No wonder the town's taprooms were the most crowded places in Hanover after working hours. Liquor was the new immigrant's tranquilizer. It provided him, in most instances, with the only release he had from the routine of his miserable existence. The only place he could express himself was among friends in one of the local taverns. When he finally returned home, often in a severe state of drunkenness, his family made sure to stay clear of him or they would meet with a violent reception.

High prices, low wages, and poor working conditions were not unique to Hanover's new immigrants. The Irish and Welsh miners of the Middle and Southern coal fields also had to contend with these same problems during the 1860s and 1870s. They responded, at various times, by violence through organizations like the Molly Maguires, an Irish fraternal society which destroyed company property, or other groups which formed unions and called general strikes. The most successful of these occurred in 1875 when the Welsh and Irish miners of the Middle and Southern anthracite fields banded together in a Workingman's Benevolent Association and refused to mine for a five-month period. Unfortunately for them, the Eastern European immigrants of the Northern field continued to work and were able to meet the nationwide demand for hard coal, forcing their coal mining brethren to the south to return to the pits at a 20 percent reduction in wages. Embittered by this turn of events, the Welsh and Irish miners developed a greater animosity toward the Lithuanians, Poles, and Russians of the Wyoming Valley, denouncing them as "strike breakers" who always seemed "to milk the cow" while the miners of the Middle and Southern fields "were left to hold the tail." Two years later when these new immigrants stopped work for three months while demanding a 25 percent increase in wages, the Irish and Welsh miners returned the favor by continuing to work.[26]

This struggle between the new immigrant miners of the Wyoming Valley and the Irish and Welsh miners to the south continued throughout the 1880s and 1890s. Not only did it prevent the unionization of the anthracite workers, but it caused a great deal of ethnic animosity between the two groups. The Irish and Welsh considered the Lithuanians and Slavs "stupid," "dirty," "ignorant," and willing to work for low wages, thereby preventing the establishment of a united mine workers union. The Lithuanians and Slavs, on the other hand, considered the Irish and Welsh to be "lazy," "elitist," and unwilling to band together in a union with unskilled laborers. This stalemate continued until 1900.

Under the dynamic leadership of young John Mitchell, the United Mine Workers Union (UMW) succeeded in organizing all four anthracite fields. In August of 1900, the UMW called a general strike to protest the arbitrary wage policies of the coal operators. After 6 weeks, the operators agreed to a ten percent pay increase in all the fields and the miners returned to work, victorious for the first time in their 40-year battle with the owners. This event strengthened the bonds between miners under UMW leadership and made possible an even more successful strike in 1902 in which the UMW was formally recognized as a collective bargaining organization by the mine owners. Nevertheless, ethnic friction continued to dominate the Wyoming Valley.[27]

Nearly two-thirds of the Wyoming Valley's population was foreign-born by 1900. Of the total force of 59,823 men who worked in the northern collieries, 36,381 were of eastern or southern European origin. And 40 percent of these were, more specifically, Lithuanian or Polish.[28] For them the process of social mobility was slow and uneven. It took years for the immigrant laborer who worked alongside an experienced miner to master the knowledge required to pass state certification so he could work independently. Further promotion to the status of mine boss, fire boss or mine foreman was almost impossible for the immigrant. Those were positions that would have to wait for the second generation. Thus, the most recent immigrants were treated the worst.

Since these recent arrivals were unskilled, they were only eligible for the position of laborer, and would not be accepted into union membership. For the Welsh and English families that owned and operated the collieries of the Wyoming Valley, they represented a cheap labor force which could be induced into working extra hours in the event of a strike by the UMW. These operators felt little remorse for the plight of their Lithuanian and Slavic workers. In fact, some genuinely believed that by providing these immigrants with work, they were doing them a great service. "They don't suffer," remarked one Welsh mine owner. "They are grateful for any work we can provide and they should be. After all, they can't even speak English and are so stupid that they can't learn the art of coal mining." If the coal operators were patronizing their new immigrant laborers, the Welsh and English miners were openly vindictive.[29]

For them, the Lithuanians and Slavs posed a serious threat to their financial prosperity. Welsh and English miners intimidated these new immigrants (often referred to as "Sclavs," a term which suggested inferiority and the friction that existed between the miner and the laborer), with both verbal and physical abuse. Beatings, pranks that often resulted in severe injuries, and property damage were common methods employed by the nativist miners in their effort to register the simple message: "Get out of town; we don't want you here!"

Peter Wyshner and many of the other Eastern European immigrants of his generation were docile. They didn't want any trouble. Instead they struggled to survive this demeaning treatment, preserving what little personal integrity they could. Their children, however, refused to tolerate the discrimination. Like Antoinette Wyshner and the minority of new immigrants who fought back, they wanted their share of the American Dream and they refused to listen to anyone who told them they couldn't have it.

Losing an Arm,
Committing to a Dream

"Growing up is a ritual—more deadly than religion, more complicated than baseball, for there seems to be no rules. Everything is experienced for the first time. But baseball can soothe over those pains, for it is stable and permanent."— W.P. Kinsella, Shoeless Joe *(1982)*

PETE GRAY WAS BORN Peter J. Wyshner Jr. on March 6, 1915, in the Hanover section of Nanticoke, the youngest of Peter and Antoinette Wyshner's five children. Like other Eastern European immigrants, the Wyshners were a close-knit family who stressed the importance of solidarity among its members. Not surprisingly, when asked by the mine boss which of his children he favored, Peter Sr. responded by raising his hand, extending the index finger and saying, "if you cut this finger the hand will hurt." Then extending the thumb, he said to his

inquirer, "and if you cut this finger the hand will hurt. My hand, sir, is
like my family and my fingers are like my children. I favor all of them."
The feelings were mutual with his children.[1]

The Wyshner children had a strong sense of obligation to the family.
They realized that their parents had worked hard and deserved all the
assistance that they could provide. To help out, the two girls, Ann and
Rose, attended school until their eighth year and then assumed most of
the domestic duties for the family. Of the three boys, Joseph was the
eldest and he assumed the responsibility for looking after Anthony who,
in turn, would look after Pete Jr., the youngest of all the children. All
three boys attended school until the age of thirteen and then went to work
at the Truesdale colliery to help support the family.[2]

When the Wyshner boys weren't working at the Truesdale colliery,
they found plenty of time for recreation. Winters were spent ice skating
on the nearby reservoir and sleigh riding down the coal banks that surrounded the colliery. Summers were filled with swimming in cave holes
and playing out in the streets with the other neighborhood children.
"Kick the ricket," "relievo," and "nip ball" were popular pastimes but,
of course, baseball was the game of choice.[3]

"Back in those days, baseball was everything," Gray would recall
years later. "There was a team on every street, seven diamonds in the
town, and kids would always be out playing."

"Besides," he added, "there wasn't much else to do. We just had a
lot of fun going to a field and playing ball from morning 'til night."[4] Since
their Eastern European immigrant parents had forbidden them to play
with anyone but "their own," the Wyshner boys played ball primarily with
the Lithuanian kids. As they grew older and met Russian, Slovak, Polish,
and Italian kids in school, their circle of friends widened. But if trouble
broke out, they were obliged to defend those of their own ethnicity. When
things got rough on the sandlots of Hanover, "you looked out for your
own," recalled John Barno, a boyhood friend of Gray's. "We were a
'rough-and-tumble' bunch of kids and it wouldn't take much for us to get
into a good fight, especially if a Welsh or English kid took you out with
a slide at second base." Barno remembers that young Pete Wyshner was
a "tough kid" but not as "overtly aggressive as he was in later years."[5]

Known to his boyhood friends as "Petey," the Wyshner's youngest
son was just like any other young boy in the Hanover section of Nanticoke
until he lost his right arm at the age of six. When that happened, he
became determined to be better than the rest. Pete lost that right arm

hitching a ride from a farmer who stopped to take him home from the west end of Nanticoke. Standing on the running board of the produce truck, he was thrown from the vehicle when the farmer had to make a sudden stop. His small body fell under the running board, his arm being mangled in the spokes of the wheel. The farmer drove Pete home and left him lying on the front porch in a fit of hysteria. When a passerby noticed how badly the young boy was hurt, she took him to the hospital where his arm was amputated above the elbow. Because Pete was naturally right-handed, it was a difficult adjustment to learn to eat and write with his left, but even more challenging to throw and hit a baseball left-handed.[6] Initially, the other kids made him a bat boy just to make him feel part of the gang. But sympathy is not what the young boy wanted. "I wanted to play ball and I knew that I had a better eye for hitting than most of those kids, I just had to learn to hit with one arm," said Gray. "So I'd go up to the railroad tracks in town, find a long stick, and throw up a rock to practice my hitting. I'd do that for hours and hours every day to develop a quick wrist."[7] For Pete, hitting was the easy part of his dilemma. Learning to field and throw with one arm would prove to be a much greater challenge.

His major difficulty was developing a method of throwing the ball immediately after he made a catch. Pete soon realized there was no way he could play in the infield. The quick change of direction and reaction time that was necessary to stop a ball hit sharply to his right would prevent him from playing any infield position effectively. But he was very capable of playing the outfield if he could find a way to release the ball from his glove quickly. Eventually he learned that by removing almost all the padding from his glove and wearing it on his fingertips with the little finger purposely extended outside of the mitt, he was able to catch the ball and get it to his throwing hand in one swift motion. He credits the success of the entire manuever to his little finger, which was bent upwards at almost a right angle. "I was bitten by a cat as a young boy," he mused, "and my finger came out crooked. If that didn't happen, I'd never have been able to play ball," insisted the one-armed baseball prodigy. "I'd catch the ball in my glove and stick it under the stub of my right arm. Then I'd squeeze the ball out of my glove with my arm and it would roll across my chest and drop to my stomach. The ball would drop right into my hand and my small, crooked finger prevented it from bouncing away."[8] Young Pete Wyshner's creativity in mastering these manuevers was only part of his success story.

"Petey was competitive in everything he did," according to Eddie Perluke, another boyhood friend. "But after he lost that arm, he wouldn't take anything from anybody." Perluke recalled one sandlot game in which the one-armed Wyshner was trying to score from second on a base hit to right field. The opposing right fielder had a strong arm and fired a strike to home plate while Pete was still yards away. The catcher, a big stocky Russian kid, had the plate blocked down the third base line and was just waiting to make the tag. Rather than accept his fate, Pete went shoulder first into the catcher laying him out on the ground. The ball trickled out of the boy's mitt and Pete was safe. When the catcher finally realized what had happened he cried out, "If it wasn't for your handicap, I'd smash your nose." He had barely completed the threat when the young Wyshner decked him again, this time with a left hook. "What handicap?" Pete retorted as he returned to the bench.[9]

"By the time I was sixteen," Gray insisted, "I was a better player than those other kids. And it wasn't because I had any more ability. It was simply because I *respected* the game more than they did. I worked damn harder than anyone else to become a good ballplayer." To be sure, the young Pete Wyshner respected others who worked hard at the game, but he had even more incentive to improve himself than they did. "When you only have one arm," he added, "you learn to take nothing for granted."[10]

Although Pete was quite an able student of baseball, he was not as motivated in the classroom. Having completed his elementary education at age thirteen, he left the McKinley School and went to work as a water-boy, first at the Truesdale colliery and later during the Great Depression for the Works Progress Administration.[11] Pete's missing arm prevented him from securing employment as a laborer in the mines like his older brothers. The Glen Alden Coal Company, which had purchased the DL & W's coal operations by the late 1920s, considered the missing arm a risk that might endanger not only Pete's life but those of others. That is why it refused to give him any employment other than carrying buckets of water for the thirsty miners. For the young Pete Wyshner, working as a waterboy was simply an "occupation"—something that occupied his time and allowed him to contribute to the family income—but playing baseball was not only his first love, it was the only thing of real meaning in his life. He followed the game just as he played it—with an unyielding passion. Professional baseball in the 1920s provided more than sufficient inspiration for an aspiring major leaguer.

The roaring twenties were a record-making time in major league baseball. It was the decade in which the Supreme Court ruled that baseball was a sport and not a business; thus was not subject to antitrust laws. It was also a decade of individual highlights: Ty Cobb collected his 3,000th hit in 1923; John McGraw, manager of the famed New York Giants, won his National League record tenth and last pennant in 1924; Rogers Hornsby of the St. Louis Cardinals compiled a .402 batting average during the five-year period between 1921 and 1925; and after a fifteen year pennant drought, the legendary Connie Mack resurrected his Philadelphia Athletics in 1929 to finish 18 games ahead of the Yankees and defeat the National League champion Chicago Cubs in a 5-game World Series. Of course, above and beyond these individual achievements, the decade of the 1920s belonged to the New York Yankees and their premier player, George Herman Ruth.

Yankee fortunes were largely built on the introduction of a livelier ball in 1921, an innovation that resulted in a 50 percent increase in home runs from the previous year. More specifically, the "Home Run Revolution" was inspired by Babe Ruth, who cracked 59 homers in '21 for the first great team of the Yankee dynasty. Two years later, in 1923, the Yankees opened a new stadium in the Bronx which was appropriately christened "The House That Ruth Built" after the Yanks defeated Boston 4–1 on an opening day home run by the Babe. In 1926 Ruth hit three round-trippers in one championship game to set a World Series single game record. And the following year, he led what has been considered the greatest team ever to play the game to a 110–44 record and a four-game sweep of the Pittsburgh Pirates for the World Series title. During that '27 season, Ruth led the major leagues in nearly every major slugging department with 60 home runs (more than any other American League *team*), 158 runs scored, 138 bases on balls, a .487 on-base percentage, and a slugging average of .772. Never had a player so completely dominated the game or captured the affection of the fans as did Babe Ruth.[12]

Like most kids in Hanover, Pete Wyshner was a Yankee fan and Babe Ruth was his hero. Rooting for Ruth and the Yankees was as patriotic as the American flag or as sacred as going to church on Sunday for the children of Lithuanian and Polish immigrants. One of Pete Gray's fondest memories was seeing Ruth's "called shot" in the 1932 Series against the Chicago Cubs at Wrigley Field. "I was 17 years old in 1932, and I hitchhiked all the way from Nanticoke to Chicago just to see that Series," he recalled. "It was quite a Series to say the least! There was some bad blood between those two teams and in game three anything could have happened."[13] New York was leading the Series two games to none. But Chicago had a die-hard attitude and fought their way back into the Series during game three.

Ruth came to bat in the top of the fifth inning with the score tied at four. Cub pitcher Charlie Root got the first pitch across the plate for a called strike, setting off a stream of jeers from the Chicago bench. When Ruth held his hand and pointed to the center field bleachers, allegedly signalling the destination of the next pitch, the Cub fans erupted in a chorus of boos and began hurling fruit at him. Ruth took the next pitch for a second strike and repeated the same gesture with his hand, earning him even more insults. Whether or not he could predict the destination of the next pitch is still the subject of much controversy, but Babe Ruth drilled the next ball deep into the center field stands and the Yankees went on to win that game 7–5 and sweep the Series. The event marked a major turning point in Pete Gray's life.

"Like most kids who loved baseball," said Gray, "I *dreamed* of playing in the major leagues, but I thought it was out of the question. After all, who ever heard of a one-armed ballplayer? But when the Babe hit that pitch into the bleachers for a home run, I said to myself, 'Pete, the whole trick is confidence in yourself. If you are sure you can do it, you will do it.'"[14] Ruth's famous if controversial "called shot" convinced a 17-year-old Pete Wyshner that he could play major league baseball. He could identify with the need to prove himself to others, especially when the challenge appeared to be nearly impossible. The one-armed adolescent returned to the sandlots of Hanover with a firm resolve to become a major league baseball player. And he approached this task with an aggressively self-confident attitude that many dismissed as "cocky." But those who knew him better understood his driving ambition to make it to the big time.

"I played semipro ball against Pete Gray in the anthracite leagues," recalled George Staller, an infielder who eventually played for the Philadelphia Athletics. "Pete was a fierce competitor who used to slide into bases with his spikes high. On one occasion, he almost got into a brawl with one of the coal miners on our team, but he wasn't the one to back away." According to Staller, Gray was also "one of the better hitters in that league, but he lacked power. That is why I was so surprised when he went into professional ball and did so well."[15]

Al Cihocki, a rookie infielder with the 1945 Cleveland Indians, followed Gray's semipro career in their hometown of Nanticoke and was much less surprised by Gray's success in the majors. "Playing ball was hard work if you wanted to turn pro," said Cihocki, "but nothing compared to working in a coal mine. When you saw your father come home every day, dead tired and for little pay, you knew you wanted something better. And Pete had the ability to make it. He was a good bunter who had the speed to steal quite a few bases." Cihocki admitted, however, that "what put Pete Gray over the top was his hard-headed determination to become a major leaguer."[16]

Everything the young ball player did was predicated on his dream of becoming a professionall baseball player. Believing that he would increase his chances to be scouted by the pros, he adopted the surname "Gray" after his brother Joseph, an amateur boxer in the Wyoming Valley.[17] A short, simple name would be easier for people to remember and perhaps even distance him from the ethnic prejudice that he experienced as the son of Lithuanian immigrants. Nevertheless, it was his Lithuanian ethnicity that got him started on his journey to the major leagues since Gray refined his skills by playing in the local Sunday leagues for St. Joseph's Lithuanian Catholic Church.

In 1924, St. Joseph's established a baseball team known as the "Lithuanian Knights." The Knights were essentially a neighborhood team which competed against other church-sponsored clubs from Hanover. To play for the Knights, the individual had to be Lithuanian and a member of St. Joseph's Catholic Church. When Gray first joined the team in 1934, however, they had become a semiprofessional organization. Prior to that year, Pennsylvania's blue laws prohibited any semiprofessional or professional club from competing on the Sabbath. The blue laws did not apply to teams such as the Knights because they were church-sponsored events conducted for the sole purpose of recreation. When teams decided to charge admission and, in some cases, pay their players, their contests were considered "professional" and, as such, subject to the Commonwealth's blue laws.[18]

In November of 1933, Pennsylvanians were asked to vote on a referendum determining whether or not the state should amend the blue laws to permit professional sporting contests on the Sabbath. The amendment passed by a vote of 1,546,619 to 729,220, and the first season of semiprofessional baseball was slated to begin in the Wyoming Valley in May of the next year.[19] Although St. Joseph's Lithuanian Catholic church continued to be an unofficial sponsor of the baseball team—which still

retained its ethnic criterion for membership—it changed its name to the
"Hanover Lits" (an abbreviation for "Lithuanians") and required its
members to pay dues amounting to 25¢ each month. Occasionally, a
"ringer" was paid to fill a void in the line-up. These were either more experienced, former minor league players who could command a price as
high as $20 a game or exceptionally talented high school athletes who
were more than happy getting $2 for the opportunity to play with the "big
boys." Their pay was secured by passing the hat among the fans during
the game.[20]

Unlike their predecessors, the Lithuanian Knights, the Lits competed against teams across the Wyoming Valley, most of which were not
sponsored by church organizations. Eight teams made up the Wyoming
Valley League: Breslau, Exeter, Glen Lyon, Hanover, Nanticoke, Power
Plant, Swoyersville, and Wilkes-Barre. Teams would play each Sunday
afternoon from May through September. Playoff berths would be determined by a club's finish in the standings. First palce would play fourth
place and second would play third in a best of three game series. The
championship would be settled in another best of three game series.
Similar arrangements existed in the other anthracite leagues of northeastern Pennsylvania. However, the outcome of these games was not as
important as the event itself for the people of Hanover.

A sunny summer Sunday became something of a ritual. After morning services, townspeople would walk home to eat their dinner and then
slowly make their way to the Lits' diamond on Mosier Street for the afternoon ball game. The players usually arrived about 12:30 to drag the dirt
infield. Pepper games, batting practice, and a quick infield warm-up
followed and the game was underway by 2:00. After the contest the
players would divide up a keg of beer and boast of their most recent
performance. It was a routine, but the most favored routine in town.
"In those days the Lits drew anywhere from two to three thousand people per game," according to John Barno, an outfielder for the great
Lits team of the mid–1930s. "Maybe it was because we had absolutely
nothing back then. There were very few cars in town so you really
couldn't go anywhere else, and there was no money since the stock
market crashed in '29 and the Depression followed. We didn't have
anything but each other and our routines. Baseball was part of that
routine. People genuinely looked forward to the game on Sunday afternoon."[21]

Indeed, the Great Depression did serve to promote popular interest in local, semiprofessional baseball. Attendance at major league baseball games plummeted from a record high of more than 10 million in 1930 to just over 6 million in 1933. The combined net income of all franchises also dropped from $1,965,000 to $217,000 during this same period. With baseball's finances approaching "the red," many cost-cutting measures were taken. Baseball commissioner Judge Kenesaw Mountain Landis took a 40 percent cut in pay, while National League president John Heydler also insisted on having his salary reduced as an example for players. The player-manager became more common during this period simply because it was cheaper to pay one man for two jobs. Naturally, the players themselves were forced to accept reduced salaries. The reserve clause binding a player to one team existed in those days, preventing free agency, and, though the players were not happy about these conditions, many were grateful just to be playing ball.[22] According to Yankee pitcher Burleigh Grimes, "The ball player is a fortunate man. In other occupations, there has been a shrinkage in salaries and lack of employment. The ball player, under terms of his contract, has gone on daily and been paid in full." Grimes was correct.[23]

Baseball players were considered "skilled laborers" at best, and yet their salaries — even with a reduction — were out of proportion when compared to those of skilled workers laboring in a year-round industry. In 1930, major league salaries were reduced to $6,000 down just $1,500 from the 1929 level. By contrast, the average earnings for a skilled worker in all industries, or at least those fortunate enough to be employed, dropped by 75 percent from the '29 level to $1,064 by 1933.[24] Simply put, the working American had to function on severely reduced wages if he had a job at all and was forced to choose between scraping up a few coins for a bleacher seat at the stadium or a meal. Since the major league stadiums nearest to the Wyoming Valley were Philadelphia's Shibe Park, New York's Yankee Stadium, or Brooklyn's Ebbets Field — all of which were a rather expensive train ride away — local baseball filled the void for the people of Hanover.

For the old men, "greenhorns," who were the earliest of the Eastern European immigrants, Sunday baseball was the highlight of their entire week. "Who ve going to play dis noon?" they would ask in broken English. When they were satisfied that their afternoon plans were still intact, they would encourage the younger men of their congregation to "play hart and vin for us because ve going to voot for you gut today!" It wasn't that these old "greenhorns" loved baseball. In fact, they would spend most of the afternoon along the right field sidelines playing cards and trying to understand what exactly was happening in the game. Entertainment was only part of it. These immigrants attended the Sunday afternoon baseball game primarily for the same reason they tried to speak English—it helped them to identify their own "Americanness," their sense of belonging to this country. For them, baseball was, indeed, the national pastime because it cut across the ethnic and socio-economic barriers that often divided them from the Welsh and English immigrants and even from other Eastern European immigrants not of their own ethnicity. They embraced the game and encouraged their children to play it because they realized that baseball was an important step in the assimilation process.

Besides, at 10¢ for admission, the game was the best bargain in town. Fans could sit anywhere they pleased, the most favored spots being the bleachers along the first base line or on the railroad tracks in deep left field. And you weren't interfering with anyone's business unless you interrupted the old greenhorns' card game along the right field line. Best of all, the people of Hanover could enjoy one of the most-favored attractions in the Wyoming Valley, their very own one-armed wonder, Pete Gray.

Nineteen thirty-four was Pete Gray's first season as a Hanover Lit. At nineteen years of age he was part of the nucleus of a young team that would take its lumps during that first year of competition. "We all started playing ball together around the age of eleven," said Gray, "and just kept playing together with the Lits." These were players like Paul Keber, Mickey Zeedock, Joe Visotski, and Eddie Sincavage, all of whom had a legitimate shot at making it to the major leagues. Each one compiled some impressive statistics in the minors, but Pete Gray was the only one to make it.

Perhaps the most tragic case was that of Paul Keber, an extremely talented left-handed pitcher. According to Gray, "Keber was one of the most outstanding pitchers I ever saw at any level of play. He hid the ball so effectively and threw so hard that you couldn't locate it until it was a few feet away from the plate." Unfortunately, Keber "threw his arm out so badly" that when his chance came for the Washington Senators in the late 1930s, he was "only half the pitcher he was with the Lits."

In his 1934 debut with the Lits, Keber fanned 12 batters and scattered 8 hits for a 7–2 victory over host Swoyersville. The next week at the Lits' home opener against Exeter, Keber struck out another 12 hitters

1934 Hanover Lits Baseball Club, Wyoming Valley Anthracite League. A 19-year-old Pete Wyshner (top row, fourth from right) stands to the right of his brother Tony. The team was known as the "Hanover Lithuanians" or "Lits" for their exclusively Lithuanian Catholic membership. (Courtesy of John Barno.)

for a 5–3 victory. In those two games, Pete Gray compiled five hits, three RBIs, scored three runs, and three stolen bases, while making some outstanding defensive plays in center field. But Gray's performances and Keber's pitching were not enough to match the more experienced teams in the league. Hanover would only earn one more victory that season, a 7–4 win against the Glen Lyon Condors. The Lits finished in last place with a 3–11 record, while Power Plant defeated Swoyersville for the title.[25]

If nothing else, the Lits' inaugural season afforded Pete Gray the opportunity to display his talent on the ball diamonds of the Wyoming Valley. He let his hitting, speed, and outfield play do most of his talking. And if that wasn't enough, his older brother Tony, who was a pitcher-third baseman for the Lits, and his mother, an avid fan, did some "talking" for him. It was not uncommon, for example, for Tony Wyshner to throw at an opposing hitter when his brother was brushed back or beaned at the plate. Tony saw this not only as an obligation to a teammate but as the unconditional responsibility of an older brother to protect his younger sibling. To this day, Pete views his late brother as the "closest friend I ever had." Not only did Tony "teach me how to play the game, but in so many ways was a role model for me."[26] Gray's teammates, on the other hand, claim that he took after his mother.

Tony Burgas, an infielder on the '34 Lits team, remembers one occasion when Antoinette Wyshner charged the mound in defense of her son. "We were playing Power Plant on our home field," he recalled, "and Pete was crowding the plate." The Power Plant pitcher "threw a few brushback pitches, but Pete—stubborn as he was—refused to budge." Burgas, who followed Gray in the batting order, knelt in the on-deck circle and watched the third pitch sail at Pete's head. "No sooner had Pete hit the deck than his mother was out on the mound pelting that pitcher with her purse," he said with a wry smile. "She was a tough customer! And there's no question in my mind that Pete developed his scrappy style of play from her."[27]

The following season the Lits jumped to the Luzerne County League, which was composed of two eight-team divisions. Hanover played in the Southern Division, which included teams from Glen Lyon, Alden, Buttonwood, Honeypot, Chauncey, Sans Souci, and Nanticoke. It managed to play only one game, a 3–1 loss against the Chauncey Reds, before being forced to withdraw from the league. Hanover's dismissal was forced by the Glen Alden Coal Company, which refused to renew the Lits' lease for use of their Mosier Street ball diamond. The action was taken by the coal company because of a miners' strike that threatened an anthracite industry already in decline.[28]

Because of Glen Alden's inability to provide full-time employment to its miners, the Auchincloss colliery was permanently closed and the Bliss colliery was open for work only 150 days of the year. Even Truesdale, the highest coal-producing operation in the Wyoming Valley, had its work schedule limited to 150 days and its work force cut in half. Angered by these developments, many of the Slovak and Lithuanian miners established a dissident union, the United Anthracite Miners of Pennsylvania (UAM), that rebelled against the United Mine Workers (UMW) leadership. The UAM believed that the UMW leaders were siding with the owners instead of acting for the welfare of the miners. The UAM demanded a policy of "job equalization" and, in 1935, went on strike to force the UMW into an agreement. Hanover became the strike front for the entire Valley because of the predominance of the Truesdale colliery.

On May 6 the town's business and professional leaders met at

Lakatos Hall and organized themselves into the Hanover Business and Professional Men's Association. Led by the Reverend Victor A. Simkonis, rector of St. Joseph's Lithuanian Catholic Church, the aim of this organization was not only to put an end to the strike but to "bring about a deeper interest in the affairs of the community from a business and civic angle." To this end, the group invited UAM leader Thomas Maloney to speak. That meeting, held on May 22, drew a crowd of over 3,000 miners and promised to put an end to the strike within the month.[29] A week later, when Maloney was killed by a mail bomb, Hanover erupted in violence.

By that time the Glen Alden Coal company had already antagonized the UAM membership by replacing them with strikebreakers — many being newly arrived immigrants who were immediately given membership in the UMW. Maloney's death was, for many of the UAM miners, the final straw. June became a month of violence in Hanover. When the UMW miners attempted to travel to work or return home, they were greeted with rocks, gunfire, and abusive language by the striking miners. According to Vincent Znaniecki, the Nanticoke chief of police, "It was a fight between two unions, something we hadn't seen before. In the past, problems had occurred between the union and the coal company. But now we were obliged to protect the UMW. All we could do was to keep them apart. I ordered my men to prevent anyone from congregating to avoid real severe violence." By June 3, Znaniecki's efforts had proved to be futile and state troopers were called into the area to escort the UMW strikebreakers to work on a daily basis. "There were 15 to 20 state policemen living in Hanover itself," recalled the police chief. "The Commonwealth rented rooms for them because our own police department needed the back up." By the end of June, the UAM was forced to concede to the UMW's policy of selective work scheduling, and the strike ended.[30]

Pete Gray vividly remembers being chased off the company-owned ball diamond even when the Lits attempted to hold an informal practice session. "The owners and the UMW were trying to spite us by refusing us the permission to use the ball field," he claimed. "They realized that many of the Lits were UAM men who refused to be intimidated by the UMW rank and file. The sad thing about it was that we had to forfeit our season since we had no diamond to play on."[31] Still the Lits managed to strike up neighborhood contests against some of the local church clubs which played in the Lithuanian Holy Name Society. It was the only way they could continue to keep their team together for the following season. Their efforts clearly paid off.

In 1936, Hanover captured the first of two consecutive Luzerne County League championships. No longer known as the "Lits," the team had opened its membership to players of Polish, Ukrainian, Russian, and Italian origin as a symbol of ethnic unity during the previous year's strike. Now known as the Hanover Athletic Association or Hanover A.A., the nucleus of the team remained Lithuanian. It was a heavy-hitting team that spent most of the season in fourth place because of its suspect defense and erratic pitching. But the team was, if nothing else, exciting to watch.

In its home opener against the Holy Cross Athletic Club of Button-wood, Hanover drew nearly 3,500 fans, the largest opening game crowd in Wyoming Valley history. It was a free-hitting contest that was decided in the eighth inning when Hanover scored nine runs on extra base hits by Stan Chetitis, Eddie Sincavage, Pete Gray, and older brother Tony Wyshner. Although Hanover won the game 17–11, its pitching allowed 15 hits and the defense committed 4 errors.[32] This would prove to be a pattern for the team as the season unfolded.

Pete Gray was the only player to go errorless for the club that season. Gray usually played center field and hit third in the line-up. He could be counted on for two or three hits each game and as many RBIs. While Gray did not have the power of the club's home run hitters, players like catcher Stan Chetitis and pitcher-first baseman Paul Keber, he was an offensive catalyst. He was a good fastball hitter who was patient at the plate and had the speed to steal a considerable number of bases. During a 16–3 rout of the Askam Athletic Club, for example, Gray led a nine-run attack in the fourth inning with two baseclearing doubles. He stretched another hit into a triple by sliding head first into third base, nearly laying out the third baseman.[33] At six feet, one-hundred and sixty pounds, Gray wasn't very intimidating, but he was hard-headed and aggressive to a fault. That quality cost him the '36 season.

During the last week of June, Hanover had the opportunity to move up from fourth place in the standings when it faced first-place Alden. The "Ace-Nines" had suffered some injuries to key players and were vulnerable to a potent offense. The game was close through eight innings but in the ninth, Alden broke a 5–5 tie with a two-run homer. Despite a 14-hit attack spurred by a Chetitis home run and a base-clearing double by Gray, Hanover lost the game in the early innings by committing five errors. Even worse, the team lost Pete Gray for the season when he

1936 Hanover Athletic Association, Luzerne County Anthracite League. Formerly known as the "Lithuanians," Hanover reorganized its club in 1936 admitting players of different ethnic backgrounds. They simplified the team's name to "Hanover Athletic Association" and proceeded to capture two consecutive league championships. Pictured above is a joint team photo of Hanover and the Askam Cubs, Pete Wyshner stands in the last row at the extreme right. (Courtesy of John Barno.)

attempted to steal third base with a head-first slide, fracturing his collar bone.[34]

　　Although Gray could hit and steal bases, he was still a raw player who needed to refine his skills, particularly his base-stealing. He did not have the balance that a two-armed individual naturally possessed. Two arms were essential for the balance and torque or upper body drive needed to be an effective baserunner. Gray made up for his disadvantage by running closer to the ground, thereby establishing a lower center of gravity. Under these circumstances, it was easier for him to dive head-first into a base, using his legs as a spring board rather than his upper body. Hanover's manager, Jack Ustar, was concerned about Gray's reckless abandon on the basepaths, especially since the Mosier Street diamond had a hard clay base and, in some spots, even rock. Ustar tried to convince Gray that he could avoid serious injury by using a hook slide. But the hard-nosed style of the anthracite leagues tended to promote the head-first slide or the feet-first slide with spikes flying high, both of which were intended to intimidate the opponent. This, of course, was consistent with Gray's outlook on life itself and so he continued to run wild, letting his more ruthless inclination take control of his body.

After Pete's injury, it was his brother Tony who led the Hanover Athletic Association to the championship. His pitching as well as his hitting made the difference for a team that, as late as August, was struggling to remain in fourth place. On August 2, Tony pitched Hanover to an 11–8 victory over the third-place Nanticoke Reds to keep his team in the chase. In that same game, the elder Wyshner went three for four with two RBIs.[35] Over the next four weeks, he would chalk up three more victories for Hanover, the most impressive being a three-hit shutout over Sans Souci, 3–0.[36] Those victories put Hanover into the playoffs against Alden, the team that not only held first place for most of the season, but had also captured the previous year's title.

Again Tony Wyshner delivered in the playoffs and Hanover swept the Ace Nines in a best of three-game series. In game one John Barno, who replaced Gray in center field, doubled home three runs in the first inning and shortstop Johnny Guzy knocked in two more in the third to give Hanover a 5–0 lead. Over the next six innings, Wyshner surrendered 3 runs on four hits, only two of them earned. Hanover won the game, 5–3, but many felt that its players performed over their heads and it was only a matter of time before Alden would prevail.[37] When the teams met again for game two the following Sunday, Hanover proved its detractors wrong.

Wyshner pitched extremely effectively, allowing only eight scattered hits. Alden's only extra base hit was a sixth inning triple which accounted for its only two runs of the game. Hanover bats erupted in the fifth inning for a total of seven runs, coming off doubles from Wyshner, Guzy, Chetitis, and Barno. The 9–2 victory was decisive, to say the least, putting Hanover into the finals against an Askam club that had finished the regular season in second place.[38] Although Hanover dropped the first game, losing by a single run in the ninth, 3–2, it clearly dominated the remaining two, 9–1 and 10–3, to claim its first Luzerne County League title.[39]

If the '36 season was a disappointment for Pete Gray, he certainly made up for it in 1937. Gray played a prominent role in virtually every game played by Hanover that season. Combining Pete's play with the pitching of his brother Tony, the Wyshner boys led Hanover to an undefeated 6–0 record through the first two months of the season. Even in defeat the Wyshners seemed to shine. In an 8–6 loss to Hillcrest, for instance, Tony struck out seven and hit a three-run homer while Pete went two for five with a double, triple, and two runs scored. It was one of only four defeats Hanover would suffer that season.[40]

Perhaps the sweetest victory for Pete came on August 20th when Hanover defeated the Lee Park Yankees and their ace McLaughlin, the premier pitcher in the Wyoming Valley. Pete was a one-man wrecking crew at the plate, accounting for four of Hanover's ten runs with two singles, a double, and a triple. The 10–4 victory sealed a first-place finish for Hanover as well as a home field advantage in the playoffs.[41] Gray's hitting and outstanding defense continued through the month of September, allowing the team to capture its second consecutive title, this one against Buttonwood.

At twenty-two years of age, Pete Gray had gone as far as he could go in the anthracite baseball leagues of the Wyoming Valley. It was time to move on to bigger and better things. Time to fulfill a burning desire to play professional baseball. Time to chase after the American Dream.

Road to the Pros

"Success in baseball requires the synthesis of a great many virtues, many of which have nothing to do with talent. Self-discipline, singlemindedness, perseverence, and ambition—these are the virtues it takes to make it to the top."—Pat Jordan, A False Spring, *(1973)*

LTHOUGH MANY people would like to take the credit for discovering Pete Gray's baseball talent, the one-armed ballplayer created his own opportunities and then made the best of them. Self-discipline, single-mindedness, perseverence, and ambition— the virtues which had inspired his parents to immigrate to the United States at the turn of the century, were the same values directing his quest to become a major league baseball player. Even with those qualities, however, it was extremely difficult for the one-armed sensation to beat the odds that stood in the way of a professional baseball career.

Opportunities in professional baseball were limited in Pennsylvania's

43

Wyoming Valley. Of the eighteen individuals who played on the Lits'
championship teams of 1936 and 1937, there were several who might
have enjoyed success in the minor leagues had they pursued a professional career. Among the most promising were power-hitting catcher
Stan Chetitis, outfielder John Barno, and pitcher Tony Wyshner. But few
of the Lits bothered to pursue the possibility. "There wasn't much money
involved in pro ball during those days," explained Barno. "You could
make a lot more money working in the mines by the late 1930s and many
of us had families to support, an obligation that wouldn't allow us to do
something that was more of a hobby than a legitimate means of employment."[1]

Of those Lits who did pursue a professional baseball career, only four
had a legitimate shot at the majors. Pitcher Paul Keber had limited success in the Washington Senators' organization, as did outfielder Eddie
Sincavage in the St. Louis Cardinals' farm system. Perhaps shortstop
Mickey Zeedock and pitcher Joe Visotski were given the best opportunities when they signed with the Wilkes-Barre Barons, a Class A
Eastern League affiliate of the Cleveland Indians. Not only did Wilkes-
Barre scrutinize the Wyoming Valley for baseball talent more carefully
than did the Scranton Miners, a Red Sox affiliate to the north, but many
players who stopped there for a summer or two jumped right to the majors without having a stint in Triple A ball. None of these Lits' players
made it to the big time, though.

Pete Gray was perhaps the least likely to succeed in his quest for a
big league career, simply because the professional scouts refused to take
a one-armed player seriously. But according to Lits teammate Tony
Burgas, the scouts not only underestimated Gray's physical abilities, but
also his heart. "If any one of us from those Lits teams of the mid-thirties
was going to make it," said Burgas, "it was going to be Pete. He loved
the game more than anything, even more than life itself. And that is
something a scout just can't evaluate — what's in a man's heart and soul."[2]

When he failed to generate any interest from the local Class A
Barons, Pete decided to market himself with as many different organizations as possible. In fact Gray spent the summer of 1938 playing for
semipro teams in Pine Grove and Scranton in the hope of getting noticed
by the Boston Red Sox. He also attended tryout camps throughout
eastern Pennsylvania in order to catch on with another professional
organization.

"The first pro team I tried out for was the St. Louis Cardinals," he said. "They held a camp in Minersville back in the late '30s. There must have been over 600 others there, and each one of us had a number on our backs. I still remember, they gave me number 48." Gray spent most of that afternoon trading stories about the semipro leagues of Pennsylvania and waiting to be called. When they finally did call, it was only to "watch me for a few minutes in the batting cage" and then to say, "'Sorry, you'll never make it in organized ball.'" Disappointed, but not defeated, Gray moved on. "What was I going to say?" he mused. "I just turned around and headed back home. That's all I could do!"[3]

A few months later, a friend gave Gray a letter of introduction to talk with Connie Mack, then owner-manager of the Philadelphia Athletics and never one to turn down a good promotion if he could afford it. Gray travelled to Philadelphia hoping for a tryout, but once again he was disappointed. "Son," Mack said, "I've got men with two arms who can't play this game." In fact, Mack's Athletics were riddled with young, inexperienced players and veterans who had already seen their heyday. He had recently broken up a team that had produced three American League pennants and two World Championships because he could not afford to pay his star players.

The Depression, with its decline in gate receipts, had taken its toll on Mack's baseball club. Signing Gray might have promoted more interest in his team in the short term, but Mack was also a man of high moral integrity. If he was going to sign a player, he wanted to be sure that the deal would figure in his plans to build a fourth championship dynasty, not to exploit a handicapped individual for the almighty dollar. Connie Mack simply did not believe that Pete Gray had the ability to enjoy a long career in Philadelphia or anywhere else for that matter. Although he never expressed those feelings directly to the one-armed ball player, Gray understood his reservations. "He never let me on the field to show what I could do though," said Pete, his voice seeming to falter at the memory. "That was the biggest problem and it just wasn't Connie Mack, it was *all* of the scouts—they'd never give me a chance to show what I could do."[4]

In 1940 Gray, determined to earn his way into organized ball, left Pennsylvania for Brooklyn, New York. He had hopes of playing for the Brooklyn Bushwicks, an outstanding semipro team whose players were often signed by pro scouts. Max Rosner, the promoter-manager of the Bushwicks, scoffed at Gray's request for a tryout. "That's the best gate-crashing stunt I've ever heard," he replied. But when the 25-year-old

Manager Connie Mack of the Philadelphia Athletics missed the opportunity to sign Pete Gray in 1938. When Gray approached him for a tryout, the legendary skipper replied, "Son, I've got men with two arms who can't play this game." (Courtesy of National Baseball Library, Cooperstown, New York.)

outfielder handed him a $10 bill saying, "keep it if I don't make good," Rosner accepted the offer. He was impressed not only with Gray's self-confidence, but with the prospect of a major gate attraction if the deal worked out. It did. That same afternoon 10,000 fans watched Gray collect two hits—one a home run—and play flawless defense in left field. After the game, Rosner returned Gray's $10 and paid him $25 more for his performance. When attendance continued to increase, Gray held out for more pay and received $350 per month for the remainder of the season, all for playing Sunday doubleheaders.[5]

Gray played for the Bushwicks for two seasons. The experience afforded him the opportunity to play against some of New York City's best white players and many legendary blacks who were members of the Municipal Baseball Association. The .350 batting average he compiled during that time also caught the eye of Jim Duffy Skelton, a scout for the Three Rivers club of the Canadian-American League who had competed against Gray in the anthracite leagues of northeastern Pennsylvania. Skelton wired Mickey O'Neill, the Three Rivers manager, about the possibility of signing Gray for the 1942 season. Although the scout boasted of Gray's ability to "run, hit, and field like a mad fool," he neglected to mention that he had only one arm.

"They signed me by telephone," recalled Gray. "When I got up to Montreal with Skelton, the manager met our train. I had a coat draped over my stump, and when I took it off, the guy almost passed out." O'Neill took one look at Gray's stump and cried, "Damn it, Skelton, what kind of a gag are you playing on me? He can't play pro ball!" But the scout assured him, "Once this kid takes the field, you'll never know that he's different from any of the others. Besides we've already signed him to a contract; we might as well give him a chance."[6]

The Canadian-American League wasn't exactly the big time. In fact, it was just a step up from semipro ball. Twenty towns participated in this Class C league during the 1930s and early 40s, eleven in the state of New York, six in the province of Ontario, two in Quebec, and one in Massachusetts. Three Rivers of Quebec province entered the league in 1941 after the Class B Provincial League folded. Known as "Les Renards de Trois Rivieres" (Three Rivers Foxes), the franchise operated independently prior to World War II, but was owned outright by the Brooklyn Dodgers after 1945. During the seven seasons that Three Rivers competed in the Can-Am League (1941–42, 1946–50), the club finished in first place only one time, 1946. The final standings usually found it in fifth or sixth place in what was then an eight-team league.[7] Nevertheless, Quebec province always seemed to draw a loyal baseball following.

"Three Rivers was a pleasant place to play," remembers hurler Ed Yasinski. "Everything looked good up there. The fans were always good to you."[8] Pitcher Bill Fennhahn agreed. "If you walked down the street one day," he said, "everybody talked to you. If you won a game the night before, well, the next day they sold standing room tickets only. And they were rabid fans. Oh, Lord! I mean everything was rah-rah for the home team and boo-boo – 'shoo,' they used to say – for the opposition. They really got you up for a game. It's too bad we couldn't win more games for them because they were fantastic fans."[9]

The fans often went to extremes to express their feelings, too. Often disapproval of an umpire's decision or a particularly poor performance by the team was greeted with flying seat cushions. At the other extreme, the player who delivered in the clutch was showered with money. Fortunately for Pete Gray, he was welcomed with open arms.

News of the one-armed wonder's arrival in Canada preceded him to the ball park, his debut proving to be something right out of the storybooks. The crowd had been calling for Gray the entire game, but it wasn't until Three Rivers was down to its last out that its wish was granted. The bases were loaded with two outs in the ninth inning and Three Rivers was trailing arch rival Quebec, 1–0, when Gray was called to pinch-hit. "It was like in the movies," Gray smiled. "The crowd went crazy. I was swinging two bats around with my arm, and they kept screaming my name in French. The count went to two and one, and I lined the next pitch down the right field line. The next thing I remember, everyone was throwing money at me. By the time I finished stooping, I'd collected over $100. Hey, I figured this game was made for me."[10] It certainly appeared that way.

Over the next week Gray went five for eight at the plate and played his left field position flawlessly. "It was amazing to see him play," said Barney Hearn, who was then with the Quebec Athletics. "He beat out a lot of bunts because he could run like hell. In fact, he could *bunt* .350 anywhere! He'd drag down first base so the pitcher would scoot over there, and then he'd bunt up the middle."[11] The Athletics quickly learned that Gray couldn't hit for distance, particularly if he was denied the fast ball, and they altered their defense to limit his success. "We knew he couldn't hit the ball over your head," admitted Hearn, "so we'd shade him in left field and throw him a steady diet of change-ups."[12] Gray learned that by adopting a more orthodox stance he could generate more bat speed as well as power at the plate. Together with his sharp eye, this new stance allowed him to overcome his weaknesses. The change resulted in more base hits, fewer strikeouts, and a considerable number of walks. Gray would also have to learn to adjust his fielding habits.

According to Hearn, Quebec baserunners knew they could take the

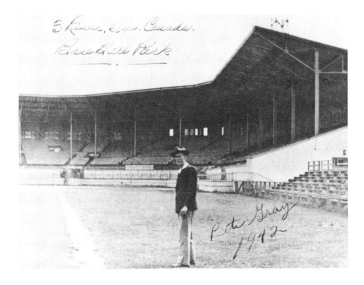

Pete Gray arrives in Three Rivers baseball park in Quebec, Canada. Later that season his hitting feats would capture the attention of the fans who would shower him with money after a particularly impressive at-bat. (Courtesy of National Baseball Library, Cooperstown, New York.)

extra base on Gray because he "needed that second or two of extra time to place the glove under his arm and roll the ball across his chest to the throwing hand. He lost a lot of runners that way." Gray soon discovered that he could reduce the time it took to field a ground ball if he simply tossed the ball up in the air, shed his glove, and then returned the ball to the infield. He also continued to perfect his maneuver for catching a fly ball so as to make it as fluid as that of a two-armed outfielder. His work ethic commanded the respect of both teammates and the opposition. "Don't misunderstand me," said Hearn in an attempt to qualify his evaluation of Gray's abilities, "Pete Gray did a terrific job for what he had."[13]

Although Gray's fast start was slowed by a fractured collarbone in late May, the result of a diving shoestring catch, he managed to return to the line-up in August. In his first game back, he went three for five, knocking in the winning run in a twelve-inning contest. The fans went wild. They hoisted Gray to their shoulders and carried their hero into the clubhouse, filling his pockets with nearly $20 in change. By the end of that season, Gray had compiled a batting average over .300.[14] This time, it was done at the professional level. Unfortunately, Pete would have to find another circuit to play in, since there would be no '43 campaign for the Canadian-American League.

American involvement in World War II put the Can-Am in mothballs. Dozens of the players were drafted or enlisted in the armed services. Those who didn't enter the service went into defense work to fill the void left on the industrial homefront. Travel restrictions made it difficult for teams to compete, particularly when they had to cross the U.S.-Canadian border so often. When attendance dropped, the owners of the league voted to curtail operations until war's end.[15] Many of those players who had hoped to stay on for the '43 season, having no prospect of climbing any further in professional baseball, returned home, ending their hopes of a major league career. Gray, however, had created enough interest to warrant the consideration of other teams at a higher level of competition.

The Toronto Maple Leafs, a Class AAA organization in the International League, purchased Gray's contract and invited him to spring training in 1943. He appeared to win over the hearts of the Toronto fans—who came out to watch him practice by the hundreds—as well as the local sportswriters. J.P. Fitzgerald, the sports editor for the *Toronto Star Weekly*, unabashedly stated that "Gray is deserving of every single break. The fact that he has gotten as far as he has, argues his earnestness, steadfastness, and gameness, and boys like that are too rare—whether in baseball or any other walk of life."

Fitzgerald's endorsement, however, was based on his admiration for Gray's personal example more than on the physical talents of a one-armed ball player and his potential for success at the triple-A level. The sportswriter anticipated the criticisms that might follow such an appeal and addressed them rather effectively. "Baseball," he wrote, "has become somewhat hard-boiled with very little sentiment in its ranks. Perhaps it is too much to expect Toronto or any other club to carry Gray or any other player very far unless they can show the goods required. Still, ball clubs have been known to waste their time on men whose supposed ability never did function because of bad habits. Gray is not in that category." Fitzgerald closed with this final pitch: "The chips have been stacked against Pete Gray and he has worked thus far against odds that would have discouraged most youths before they started. Here's hoping the youngster may make Toronto or some other team. He deserves all the encouragement that can be given him."[16] Burleigh Grimes, the Toronto manager, felt otherwise.

Gray survived the first cut of the training camp in mid–April, but was released shortly after. He was ill and felt that he hadn't been given a fair chance. Another account claims that Gray angered Grimes by comparing the manager's knowledge of the game with that of Mickey O'Neill, his former pilot at Three Rivers, for whom Gray had tremendous respect. When Grimes learned of the criticism, he supposedly got his revenge by releasing Gray.[17] Regardless of the circumstances, Pete Gray would have to find himself another team for the '43 season, and preferably in the United States. At the same time, his experience in Canada confronted him with a serious personal dilemma.

Although the statistics he compiled at Three Rivers seemed proof enough that Pete Gray had the ability to compete at a higher level, his release by Toronto coupled with the charitable – albeit well-intentioned – remarks he was getting in the press, began to work on his self-esteem. By birthright he was a fighter, the son of Lithuanian immigrants who had felt the sting of ethnic discrimination by an anthracite aristocracy. He realized that he had already beaten the odds that destined most of his neighbors to a future in the coal pits by going beyond the mountains of Pennsylvania's Wyoming Valley and proving that he could earn a dollar at something other than mining. Not only had he conquered a fear of the unknown, but also a very real personal fear that a one-armed ball player could never make it outside the sandlots of northeastern Pennsylvania. By playing for Three Rivers, he had done all that and more. And yet Pete Gray's burning desire to play major league baseball would not allow him to become complacent with those achievements.

Gray's almost pathologic fear of failure motivated him to do better. If he enjoyed the success he had with Three Rivers at the Class C level, then surely he could make it at the next level of baseball competition. He had to. The alternative was returning to Hanover as a failure and working at something for which he had little or no interest. Under those circumstances, Pete Gray would be just like everyone else. Deep down, that is what he feared most. That is why he vowed to do better, to become a "somebody" at something for which he had the talent. Above all, Gray wanted his success to come on his own terms.

Pete Gray wanted to make it to the major leagues because he *deserved* to make it, not because someone was kind-hearted enough to help a cripple or because he could provide a franchise with a lucrative curiosity item that would attract large crowds. His basic sense of integrity wouldn't allow for anything less. Consequently, he would struggle with his desire to be judged on his baseball skill—to be respected for his integrity as a professional athlete—and the tendency of others to treat him like a "charity case" or a "freak show."

Had Grimes actually done Gray a favor by cutting him from the Maple Leafs? Was he sparing Gray the personal humiliation he might very well suffer if he made it to a higher level of baseball competition? Did a one-armed player actually have the ability to go any further in professional baseball? These were questions that could only be answered over the course of the next few years.

Baseball Goes to War

"We're fighting for a lot of things in this war, and baseball is one of them."—A wounded American soldier (1944)

D URING THE SUMMER of 1941 the attention of most Americans focused on three things: Joe DiMaggio's fifty-six game hitting streak, Ted Williams' .406 batting average, and the worsening international crisis in Europe and the Far East. All three events seemed to capture the imagination of the public, though clearly not with the same emotional impact. DiMaggio and Williams, with their graceful performances, were challenging the history of our national pastime. They evoked suspense and awe among the fans as well as nostalgic memories of the great ones who had gone before them. By the end of the '41 season, the Yankee Clipper and the Splendid Splinter had changed the game forever, setting standards that no one has since reached.[1]

Adolf Hitler's quest for a totalitarian dictatorship, on the other hand, evoked fear and bitter animosity among the American people, the

53

majority of whom sought to distance themselves from the Nazi atrocities. December 7, 1941, changed all that. The Japanese attack on Pearl Harbor quickly dispelled whatever isolationist sentiment existed in the United States. It united the country in a way that nothing else could have done. It also changed the lives of an entire generation, giving them a profound understanding of qualities that became part of the national character—sacrifice, courage, and patriotism. They were also the qualities that characterized the men who shaped the national pastime during this era.

Not long after the attack on Pearl Harbor, baseball players began to enlist in the armed forces. They did not seek any special treatment, but accepted their responsibilities as American citizens to defend their country in a time of war. Their absence not only reduced the major leagues of quality performers but raised serious questions about whether or not the game would even continue.

The exodus of first-class players, along with the concern that transporting the 16 major league clubs around the country would divert natural resources necessary for the war effort, led Baseball Commissioner Kenesaw Mountain Landis to consider suspending major league play during the war. Reluctant to begin the 1942 season only to have it disbanded, Landis wrote to President Franklin D. Roosevelt seeking advice. "Baseball is about to adopt schedules, sign players, make vast commitments, and go to training camps," he informed the president. "What do you want it to do? If you believe we ought to close down for the duration of the war, we are ready to do so immediately. If you feel we ought to continue, we would be delighted to do so. We await your order."[2]

The president's response was immediate and encouraging. He believed it imperative to continue major league play, something he considered essential to national morale. "I honestly feel that it would be best for the country to keep baseball going," he wrote. "There will be fewer people unemployed and everybody will work longer hours and harder than ever before. And that means that they ought to have a chance for recreation and for taking their minds off their work even more than before."

Roosevelt's "green light," however, came with the strongly worded suggestions to extend night games "because it gives an opportunity to the day shift to see a game occasionally," and to persuade all those players who were physically capable to enlist in the armed services. "As to the players themselves," wrote Roosevelt, "I know you agree with me that individual players who are of active military or naval age should go, without question, into the services. Even if the actual quality of the teams is lowered by the greater use of older players, this will not dampen the popularity of the sport."[3]

FDR's directive only reinforced what had already become government policy under the Selective Service Act passed by Congress during the prewar preparations of 1940. According to this act, men 18 through 45 years of age were required to register but only those between the ages of 20 and 32 would actually be called to serve in the armed forces. The act was revised by Congress in November of 1942, allowing for the conscription of men 18 and 19 years of age. Draft deferments were to be based on the number of dependents a man had and the extent to which his civilian job contributed to the war effort. Single men with no dependents were the first to be drafted. Second to go were single men with "collateral" dependents such as parents but without a job that contributed to the war effort. Third were single men with collateral dependents and with a job that did contribute. Fourth in the hierarchy were married men without children and without a contributing job. Fifth were those men who were married without children but with a contributing job. Sixth were married men with children but without a contributing job. And seventh were married men with children and with a job that contributed to the war effort. Although local draft boards determined which jobs were essential to the war effort and standards varied from community to community, as did the number of men available to meet the local draft quotas, those jobs considered "essential" generally included: chemists, coal miners, commercial fishermen, dairy and livestock workers, farmers, firemen, medical and law students, merchant seamen, physicians, policemen, state legislators, and teachers. Of course, "professional baseball player" was not among the essential occupations.[4]

Among the 12 million Americans who went to war during the period from 1942 to 1945, there were 500 major league baseball players and nearly 4,000 minor leaguers. The majority of these men enlisted, refusing to accept any special treatment because of their professional athletic status or even a deferment that was warranted due to their personal circumstances.[5] Ted Williams, for example, joined the Navy after a '42 campaign in which he captured the American League triple crown with a .356 average, 36 home runs, and 137 runs batted in, despite the fact that he was the sole support for his mother.[6] Joe DiMaggio, who compiled an impressive .333 average in the '42 Fall Classic, also enlisted even

though he had a 3-A classification, being married with a child at the time.[7] Both players gave up three years of their baseball prime in order to serve their country. Other star performers went to war, too. Among them were Tommy Henrich, Phil Rizzuto, and Red Ruffing of the New York Yankees; Pee Wee Reese and Pistol Pete Reiser of the Brooklyn Dodgers; Bob Feller of the Cleveland Indians; and Charlie Gehringer, Hank Greenberg, and Birdie Tebbetts of the Detroit Tigers. Perhaps the most unfortunate timing came for Hank Greenberg.

This page and previous: Reluctant to begin the 1942 season because of U.S. involvement in World War II, Baseball Commissioner Kenesaw Mountain Landis sought advice from President Franklin D. Roosevelt who gave him a "green light" to begin the season. (Courtesy of National Baseball Library, Cooperstown, New York.)

Greenberg was at the height of his baseball career when he was drafted 19 games into the 1941 season. He had already established himself as a superstar slugger, having captured the American League's Most Valuable Player award twice, collecting a total of 249 home runs in eight seasons with the Tigers. Detroit, which had lost the 1940 World series in seven games to the Cincinnati Reds, had every intention of repeating as American League champs in '41 and pinned its hopes on another productive season by Greenberg. Its plans never materialized. Although a military physician noted that Greenberg had flat feet— something that should have qualified him as a 4-F deferment—he was declared 1-A, physically fit for military service, and ordered to report to Fort Custer, Michigan, for basic training. "I never asked for a deferment," admitted the Tiger slugger. "I made up my mind to go when I was called. My country comes first. Besides it wasn't as much of a sacrifice as it appeared at the time. It was a one-year draft, and war hadn't been declared yet. I thought I'd return for the 1942 season."[8] Little did Greenberg know that he wouldn't return for four and a half years.

Hank Greenberg was released from military service on December 5, 1941. He had been in uniform for eight months, advancing in rank from private to sergeant and proving to be quite a capable soldier. Moreover, his sense of patriotism had become even stronger through the experience. That is why Greenberg was the first major leaguer to enlist after the attack on Pearl Harbor, knowing full well that he might never play major league baseball again. His farewell to the majors was short and simple: "I'm going back in. Our country is in trouble and there is only one thing to do—return to service. Baseball is out the window as far as I'm concerned. I don't know if I'll ever return to it."[9]

For Pete Gray, there was no choice—even though he was more than willing to put his professional baseball career on hold for the war effort. Gray tried to enlist shortly after the Pearl Harbor attack, but the local draft board refused to take him because of the missing right arm. He was classified 4-F, physically unfit for military service, and sent home. "I never deserved the 4-F classification," he said bitterly, recalling the experience years later. "If I could teach myself to play baseball with one arm, I sure as hell could handle a rifle or anything else the military threw my way!"[10] Gray took the rejection personally, refusing to acknowledge that any young man with a missing arm or leg was automatically exempted from military service. It was the law, and nothing would change that. In fact, the 4-F status turned out to be a blessing in disguise.

The war stripped the major leagues of some of its finest talent. Clubs were forced to search for 4-Fs like Pete Gray and Bert Shepard, a fighter pilot who lost his leg in the war and returned home to pitch one game for the Washington Senators. Those ballplayers ineligible for military service because of their age also had a better opportunity to make it to the majors. Pepper Martin, who retired after the 1940 season, was reactivated by St. Louis at the age of 40 and helped lead the Cardinals to the 1944 World Series. At the other extreme was Joe Nuxhall, a 15-year-old pitcher who was signed to a Cincinnati Reds' contract in 1944. Although he pitched only two-thirds of an inning and left with an earned run average of 67.50, Nuxhall eventually returned to the majors to win 135 games.

Shepard, Martin, and Nuxhall realized that their wartime careers occurred because of the depletion of talent in the majors. They accepted that fact and enjoyed the opportunities they had been given. "Losing my leg in the war created the publicity which helped give me the opportunity to play in the majors," admitted Shepard. "I didn't care how I got into the ballpark, as long as I got a chance to play."[11] Similarly, Nuxhall claims that he considered the experience a real novelty. "Appearing in a major league baseball game at age 15 was an awesome experience. I was able to sit on the bench with my boyhood idols and, if nothing else, I had a good seat for the game," he said.[12] Pete Gray was not as objective about his own circumstances.

Gray was in his mid– to late–twenties during World War II. He had been struggling his way up the "baseball ladder" from semipro to double A ball for nearly a decade. It had not been easy for him. While he could stomach the idea of reactivating Pepper Martin and even giving Bert Shepard a shot at big league ball, Gray had trouble understanding Nuxhall's immediate entry into the big time. After all, Martin had once been a bona fide major league player, and though Shepard could not boast of the same credentials, the fighter pilot had paid his dues in the minor leagues for several years before going off to war and becoming a hero. Gray could respect these men. They had established their own professional identities and deserved their success. It was more difficult however, to understand the 15-year-old Nuxhall's sudden rise to the majors.

Pete Gray was a mature young man looking to establish his professional identity as a legitimate major league baseball player. If anything, the teenager's wartime stint in the majors diminished the integrity of the sport. Nuxhall was pitching for his high school team just three weeks before he appeared in a major league game. He had no minor league experience to prove himself to veterans who had labored in the farm system for years. Gray could not help but wonder if the Reds actually believed this youngster had the ability to compete on the major league level. If he didn't, then why was he in the majors? As a novelty?[13] Either way, Nuxhall's inning of glory cheapened Gray's lifelong dream of becoming a major league ballplayer. Still, there were those who suffered an even greater disadvantage than Gray.

At the outset of World War II, the color barrier still existed in professional baseball as well as in the United States military. African American baseball players competed in their own Negro leagues, which by war's end proved to be every bit as competitive — if not more so — than the major leagues. Many of the Negro leagues' top players remained home and continued to play during the war, primarily because they could not enlist until 1942 or were too old to join up after that time. Satchel Paige, who pitched at least 23 no-hitters, Josh Gibson, who came as close as anyone to hitting a ball out of Yankee Stadium and Cool Papa Bell, who ran the 100 yard dash in 9.6 seconds, were well into their thirties at the time of the war, which prevented them from joining up. According to Harrington Crissey, author of *Teenagers, Graybeards, and 4-F's*, with players like Gibson, Paige, and Bell, "the best of the black clubs could have given the best of the white clubs a tussle any time, and that was more so during the war."[14] These were the men who were quickly becoming the marquee names in the sport since white baseball on the homefront suffered from a lack of talent.

Richard Goldstein, author of *Spartan Seasons: How Baseball Survived the Second World War*, estimates that of 128 ball players who were everyday starters in 1945, only 32 were regulars in 1946. That means that 96 players who regularly started games during the '45 season were either too old, too young, or too physically disabled to serve in the armed services. They also made nearly 1,500 errors more than usual during that season alone. No wonder attendance figures dropped from 10 million in 1941 to a low of 7.7 million in 1943.[15] Most bona fide big leaguers were playing in olive drab and khaki.

At Hickam Field in Pearl Harbor, Hawaii, the Seventh Army Air Force had a former or future major leaguer at every position, its premier player being Joe DiMaggio. The Navy became so frustrated with losing to this team that Admiral Chester W. Nimitz, Commander of the Pacific

Fleet, ordered the Navy's best players from all over the world brought to Hawaii for the 1944 Service World Series. Newspapers hailed the 10-game showcase—won by the Navy, 8 games to 2—as the "real '44 World Series."[16] The only other even to have captured more attention than the Service World Series was the 1942 Army-Navy All Star game played in Cleveland, an event which drew more than 62,000 fans.[17] Although baseball on the homefront may have lacked the luster of its peacetime superstars, it still made a major contribution to the war effort.

Baseball proved to be a cornerstone of the government's campaign to rally Americans behind the war effort, specifically in its attempt to keep the war alive in the minds of the people. To this end, a number of measures were adopted by the major leagues. For example, the national anthem was played for the first time on a regular basis before each game. Servicemen were often admitted to games free of charge. Players took ten percent of their salaries in low-interest war bonds.[18] Dozens of benefit games were held to raise money for the USO, the Red Cross, and Army and Navy relief agencies. In fact, between 1942 and 1944, each of the 16 major league franchises promoted at least one home game a year as a benefit to aid the families of servicemen. Altogether, organized baseball contributed $2,900,000 to charities during World War II. Baseball even broke into the movie industry.[19]

The motion picture was the most important leisure activity for many Americans during the World War II era. Often the feature presentation was preceded by a newsreel that offered a visual synopsis of the war news and one that always showed American involvement in the most favorable light. It was common to show a clip of a Bob Feller, Joe DiMaggio, or Hank Greenberg in military uniform to reinforce a patriotic commitment to baseball heroes, apple pie, and the United States. Perhaps the greatest impact baseball had at the box office, though, was the 1942 release of *Pride of the Yankees*, the life story of Lou Gehrig. The legendary Yankee hero, who had died a year earlier at age 37 of amyotrophic lateral sclerosis, reminded Americans of a very sad but profound truth, namely that even heroes can die young.[20]

In addition to these patriotic measures, professional baseball also accepted a fair share of sacrifices during the war. Thirty-two minor league clubs were forced to suspend their operations altogether, unable to meet their modest payrolls and unwilling to tax the transportation systems and oil reserves that were needed for the war effort. Fuel resources were protected with such great care that the military even imposed coastal "dimouts" in order to prevent the possibility of oil tanker sinkings by German U-boats that might find their way into U.S. waters. Consequently, only one hour of artificial light was allowed at New York's Polo Grounds and Brooklyn's Ebbets Field, homes of the Giants and Dodgers respectively. Evening games began in daylight and ended under the lights, sparking a popular innovation known as the "twilight game."[21] Transportation raised a similar concern. In December of 1942, Joseph B. Eastman, director of the Office of Defense Transportation, asked Baseball Commissioner Landis to meet baseball's travel requirements "without waste in space or mileage" since the demands of the war threatened to exhaust the nation's railroads. Landis responded by ordering all sixteen major league teams to conduct their spring training north of the Mason-Dixon line and revised their schedules so a team would visit each of its seven competitors three times during the season rather than the customary four. Instead of basking in the bright Florida sun, major league teams such as the Chicago Cubs, Cincinnati Reds, Detroit Tigers, and Cleveland Indians found training sites in Indiana. Others, such as the Boston Red Sox, Philadelphia Phillies, and Washington Senators used the training facilities at nearby colleges or prep schools.[22] "The amount of miles they saved by not going to Florida was insignificant," claims Richard Goldstein, "but it would not have looked good in the papers for baseball players to be lounging on the beaches while marines were dying on Guadalcanal."[23] Perhaps the most creative response to wartime needs was the introduction of the infamous "balata ball."

Although patriotic fans tossed back some 148,644 foul balls in order to conserve on rawhide and rubber, major league baseball was faced with a serious baseball shortage at the start of the '43 season due to the lack of rubber cores. The A.G. Spaulding Company responded to the shortage by introducing the "balata ball," the core of which was manufactured from the gummy juice of the tropical balata plant. Unfortunately for Spaulding, the ball proved to be so dead that 11 of the first 29 major league games played with it resulted in shutouts. Not surprisingly, the balata ball was extremely unpopular with the hitters as well as the fans, and it disappeared almost as quickly as it surfaced.[24]

Balata balls, dimouts, and 4-Fs aside, wartime baseball still retained the excitement and glory of yesteryear. In 1942 the St. Louis Cardinals tallied 106 victories to clinch the National League flag, beating out the Dodgers by 2 games. The Yankees, on the other hand, clinched the American League by a wider 9 game margin over the Boston Red Sox.

The Yankees were still the most dominant team in the game, having lost only four games in their five World Series appearances since 1936, and they were heavily favored to win the '42 Fall Classic. But '42 would prove to be a time of firsts.

The '42 Series was the first to be broadcast around the world by shortwave radio; the proceeds went, in part, to the Army Emergency Relief Fund. It was also the first time Stan "the Man" Musial, an individual who was one of the best pure hitters in baseball and an indispensable part of the Cards' line-up for years to come, appeared in World Series competition. And it was the first time the St. Louis Cardinals had faced the Yankees in the World Series since the Bronx Bombers defeated them in a four-game sweep in 1928.

When the Yankees defeated the Cards 7–4 in the opening game in St. Louis, it appeared as if the New Yorkers were on their way to capturing a record ninth world championship. But the tide turned in game two when St. Louis clinched a 4–3 victory behind the pitching of 24-year-old Johnny Beazley. The Cards went a game up in the Series when southpaw Ernie White tossed a six-hit shutout at Yankee Stadium. The following day the Cards outslugged the Bronx Bombers, 9–6, and clinched the championship in game five, again on the arm of Beazley. It was a major World Series upset, the first defeat for the Yankees in the Fall Classic since 1926. Both clubs repeated as pennant winners in '43, but this time the Yankees won the Series in five games. Shortly after the close of the '43 season, *The Sporting News*, in its summary of the most recent campaign, conceded that the "Allies could win the war without baseball, but the path to triumph would be longer, and for those on the home front, certainly much more onerous."[25] It was, indeed, correct.

Americans were being asked to sacrifice on the battlefield as well as on the home front. The government placed limits on food, clothing, and other essentials. Ration books were issued for meat, butter, coffee, and canned foods. Gasoline was restricted to four gallons per week for most, an amount considered sufficient for "necessary driving" such as shopping, getting to work, and trips to the doctor or to church. Only those who were employed in war-related industries, as well as physicians, were entitled to a bit more than the standard gas ration. Secretary of Agriculture Claude Wickard encouraged Americans to plant "victory gardens" in order to meet the nation's growing food needs. Gardens, usually consisting of corn, tomatos, beans, and peas, began sprouting up in backyards across the country. By 1944, victory gardens accounted for

forty percent of all vegetables grown in the United States. The greatest
sacrifice, however, was given by those families who sent their sons off to
war, never to return again. They lived in homes which displayed a white
satin flag trimmed in a red and gold border and highlighted by a gold
star, signifying the death of a son—an American serviceman who had
given his last full measure of devotion to his country. When a passerby
saw that flag, it was difficult to dismiss the fear that the next gold star
could represent someone in his own family. It was a fear that was reinforced on a daily basis when Americans opened their local newspapers
and read the casualty lists coming in from Europe and the Pacific.[26]

It was hard to believe that baseball—or anything for that matter—
meant much to Americans under those circumstances, but it did; and the
men who played the game became, in a very personal way, heroes on
the home front. Bill Gilbert, author of *They Also Served*, reminds us that
the kids, old timers, and 4-Fs who "really kept baseball alive for our national morale—and for our fighting men overseas—weren't the greatest
players fans ever paid to see, but for four seasons beginning in 1942 they
were our favorites. They were the ones whose exploits we cheered, whose
shortcomings we overlooked, and whose contributions to the war effort
qualified them to feel that, in a manner considered important even by
the President, they also served."[27] Pete Gray was one of those special
individuals.

MVP of the
Southern Association

"Boys, I can't fight. And so there is no courage about me. Courage belongs on the battlefield, not on the baseball diamond. But if I can prove to any boy who has been physically handicapped that he, too, can compete with the best—well, then, I've done my little bit."—Pete Gray to Philadelphia sportswriters who honored him as the Most Courageous Athlete of 1943

A FTER HIS RELEASE by Toronto in March of '43, Pete Gray spent the remainder of spring training trying to sign on with another club. Mickey O'Neill, Gray's manager at Three Rivers, lent his support to the one-armed outfielder by contacting both minor and major league clubs in an effort to get him a tryout. Their efforts were futile.

"No amount of talking helped sell Pete," recalled O'Neill. "I have to admit that I was really discouraged for him. We must have approached a dozen clubs on the East Coast and in the South just looking for a tryout. They'd invite us to camp but never took Pete seriously." O'Neill and Gray went from camp to camp putting on what amounted to little more than a "dog and pony" show. O'Neill would throw batting practice and hit fly balls while Gray put on a demonstration that would astonish the small crowds who gathered to watch their team's annual spring ritual.

"It was really something to see," according to O'Neill. "I'd toss 'em over the plate to Pete and he'd clout 'em to all fields, left, right, center. Then he'd go into the outfield and I'd chase him all over those green cow pastures with fungoes, high, far, and wide. And Pete caught 'em all. I'd marvel at the skill of this lad who'd been—I don't like to use the word— crippled. And yet he certainly didn't play like any cripple. He was better than 19 of 20 men his age, weight, and training," insisted the former Canadian pilot. "So there I was with Pete roaming the outfield like Tris Speaker and Joe DiMaggio rolled into one. I'd look around and not a damn person from the club was there to watch him. Absolutely nobody took the trouble to watch him work out. My heart went out to that kid."[1]

In mid–April, with no possibility of catching on with a team, Gray returned to Hanover. Word of Gray's alleged tiff with Toronto manager Burleigh Grimes had gotten around the professional circuit and the message was loud and clear: no one wanted a troublemaker on his roster, no matter how talented he was. Fortunately for Gray, O'Neill, who continued to contact clubs, convinced Manager James "Doc" Prothro of the Memphis Chicks that Gray would be a "good risk to take." A week later, the one-armed player received a telegram from Memphis informing him that he had secured a place on the Chicks' roster.[2] Within the hour, Gray was packed and ready to head south. He would find Memphis much to his liking.

Memphis sits on the lower Chickasaw bluff overlooking the Mississippi River in the extreme southwest corner of Tennessee. Traditionally known for its cotton and hardwood lumber markets, by the 1940s these industries had attracted increasing numbers of northerners, boasting a population of nearly 300,000. Although Memphis was considered the leading metropolis of the mid–South, the city still retained a cozy, small-town atmosphere. Much like those of the Wyoming Valley of Gray's youth, the people were friendly and hard-working, and they were strongly devoted to their baseball team, the Memphis Chickasaws, more commonly known as the "Chicks."

Named for an Indian tribe that was indigenous to southern Tennessee, the Chicks were one of more than 300 minor league teams that competed in 60 different leagues throughout the United States, Canada, and Mexico in the early '40s. This was before the reorganization of the minor league structure in 1962. Under the revision, the number of leagues declined to 20 in about 130 cities. Leagues were reclassified from their traditional A, B, C, and D designations based strictly on ability into AAA (Triple A), AA (Double A), A and Rookie leagues determined by talent as well as population. Player contracts—once the most valuable operating asset of the minor league clubs—were virtually all owned or controlled by parent major league clubs. In the 1940s, the Chicks were a strictly local institution. Memphians had owned and operated the team from its establishment in 1901 as a charter member of the Southern Association, and they enjoyed a proud history of success.

The Southern Association was the highest-ranking circuit in the South with teams in Birmingham, Chattanooga, Little Rock, Memphis, Nashville, New Orleans, Shreveport, and Selma (later Atlanta). Memphis, in particular, had a reputation for producing major league talent, having been the training ground for Hall-of-Famers Luke Appling, Billy Herman, and Dazzy Vance as well as other distinguished players, including Billy Southworth, Ted Kluszewski, and Paul Cobb. The 1924 team, which compiled 104 victories (one shy of setting a new Southern Association record at the time), set a standard for the Chicks who regularly finished in the first division. During the 1940s much of that success was due to the managerial skills of James T. Prothro.[3]

Prothro enjoyed a brief but fairly respectable career in the 1920s as a third baseman for the Washington Senators, Boston Red Sox, and Cincinnati Reds. After retiring, he became the manager of the Chicks for thirteen seasons, a period that was interrupted by a brief interlude in which he managed the Philadelphia Phillies to three successive last-place finishes in 1939, '40, and '41. He enjoyed greater success with the Chicks where he captured a pennant in 1930 and kept them in contention for nine of his twelve seasons at the helm. A strict disciplinarian, Prothro endeared himself to his players by looking out for their best interests. More affectionately known as "Doc" because of his off-season dentistry practice, Prothro actively politicked to generate major league interest in his players and gave them tips on how they could draw big league attention to themselves.

"When I arrived in Memphis," recalled Gray, "Prothro liked what he

One-Armed Wonder of the Southern Association, Gray joined the Memphis Chicks in 1943. A year later he was voted MVP of the Southern Association for compiling a .333 average while collecting 119 hits for 221 total bases and driving in 60 runs. His .996 fielding percentage and 336 put-outs led all Southern Association outfielders and his 68 stolen bases tied the all-time league record. (Courtesy of AP/Wide World Photos.)

saw in me. He gave me a chance when a lot of other clubs wouldn't trust a one-armed player. Before I signed my contract, he told me to add a few years on to my birthdate so I would appear to be younger than I actually was. Then when the big league clubs saw the roster I was listed as a twenty-six-year-old player instead of the twenty-nine-year-old I actually was."[4] It was a shrewd move. Prothro realized that, with most of the major league talent at war, many older "graybeards" with big league experience were coming out of retirement to play in the majors again. He knew that Gray would better his chances of making the big time if he appeared to be three years younger than he actually was. Nevertheless, Gray preferred to let his bat and glove do their own talking.

In one of his first appearances at the Chicks' Russwood Park, Gray put on a hitting display against the Nashville Volunteers that raised eyebrows across the Southern Association. In the first inning he doubled to center. In the fourth he beat out a bunt. In the sixth he lined a single to left. Then, in the ninth with the bases loaded, the Nashville outfield shifted to left when he came to bat. Undeterred by the switch, Gray promptly lined to right, scoring two runners. His performance on the basepaths and in the outfield was just as aggressive.

Gray went out of his way to bait rival players and challenge umpires, regarding the men in blue as "square heads in round masks." It was the only way he knew how to play the game, the way he had learned in the anthracite leagues of Pennsylvania's Wyoming Valley. At times his gritty style made him unusually vulnerable to injury. In every game Gray would chase after a ball that another outfielder wouldn't take a chance on, and he often came up with breathtaking catches, throwing runners out at the plate on a number of occasions. Chicks fans idolized him, calling him their "One-Armed Wonder." And with such a ruthless style of play, Gray quickly established himself as one of the Southern Association's most spirited, rough-and-tumble performers.

In mid–May Gray sprained a finger going after a tough ground ball. Prothro tried to convince Gray that a week's rest would do him good, but the "One-Armed Wonder" refused to rest, believing that he would let down the fans by doing so. He was correct. According to Prothro, "The fans just wouldn't let Pete alone. I'd have half a dozen calls each day wanting to know if I was going to play him—and it was the same every day wherever we travelled, not just in Memphis."[5] But even Prothro began to question the wisdom of playing his star outfielder every day. In '43, the Chicks were going absolutely nowhere in the standings, and Gray, who insisted that he play every day in order to "carry my load," refused to give less than his usual 100 percent. It took a game against Birmingham in mid–June to get him out of the line-up. In the span of three innings Gray managed to tear open his left hand and injure his knee on the basepaths; still he tried to hobble out onto the field for the fourth. Prothro put his foot down, and Gray was forced onto the disabled list for ten days. Subsequently, Gray learned to distinguish more carefully between "toughing it out" and sheer ignorance. Nevertheless, it was his diehard attitude that endeared Pete Gray to his manager. Prothro appreciated Gray's efforts and took advantage of every opportunity to boast of his star outfielder's abilities in the press.

"Gray can do everything a two-armed player can do and maybe a lot more," said Prothro. "He can hit the ball where they ain't — and there isn't a better outfielder in any league." Exceptional ability was only part of the story Prothro told. The Chicks' pilot carefully planned his interviews when asked about Gray, to appeal to the gate interests of prospective major league teams by adding, "If there is one guy who could pack them in the big leagues, to beat Babe Ruth as a drawing card, his name is Pete Gray."[6]

Prothro also alleviated any questions there might be about Gray's personal disposition. Many big league clubs still remembered the alleged incident with manager Burleigh Grimes, in that Toronto had led to the outfielder's release. Additionally Gray's insistence that he be treated as a professional major league prospect, and not as a "freak show" because of his missing arm, led to concerns about his ability to deal with that issue personally as well as publicly. Accordingly, Prothro always seemed to underscore Gray's wonderful sense of humor, pointing out that the One-Armed Wonder could laugh about his missing limb. Prothro's personal favorite was a story about one of Gray's female admirers, a motherly fan who expressed her concern about the outfielder's missing right arm.

"One hot afternoon after we won a close game," said the Chicks' manager as he recalled the incident on yet another occasion, "Pete was jogging for the locker room to take a cold shower when a lady fan reached over the runway and grabbed him by the shoulder.

"'Oh, you poor boy,' she said, 'playing baseball with just one arm and running and throwing and swinging that bat so hard. It must be an awfully tough job for you.'

"She kept running on like that for three or four minutes. Pete was getting tired of waiting for his shower, but he stuck it out.

"'And how did you lose your right arm, you poor boy?' she finally asked.

"'A lady in Brooklyn talked it off, ma'am,' Pete responded, and raced off to the showers."[7]

In 1943 the Chicks finished last in the league, compiling a 56–81 record, but it was a tremendous success for Gray. In 126 games, he captured national attention by collecting 131 hits, 42 RBIs, and hitting for an average of .289.[8] His example gave hope to dozens of American servicemen who returned home from the war as amputees. Gray seemed to embody the American underdog who could beat the odds on a regular basis because of sheer confidence, guts, and discipline. Not surprisingly, his aggressive play won the respect of the Philadelphia sportswriters, who honored him as the Most Courageous Athlete of the Game. With characteristic humility, Gray, when presented with the award, downplayed his personal struggle to become a professional baseball player and spoke instead of his tremendous respect for the American soldiers fighting abroad.

Acknowledging his responsibility to those soldiers, he told the sportswriters: "Boys, I can't fight. And so there is no courage about me. Courage belongs on the battlefield, not on the baseball diamond. But if I can prove to any boy who has been physically handicapped that he, too, can compete with the best—well, then, I've done my little bit."[9] The response would become a trademark for Gray, who never really felt comfortable with his instant rise to fame or the issue of the soldier-amputee. He was basically a shy person who wanted to be left to his own business which was playing professional baseball, but the press and the public would not allow him that luxury.

The War Department made movies of the one-armed outfielder at play in order to rejuvenate the spirits of amputees in veterans hospitals. Newsreels depicted his creative fielding technique for theater audiences across the nation, and feature articles appeared in *Time*, *The Saturday Evening Post*, and *The Sporting News*. Gray responded as best he could out of a personal responsibility he felt to the American soldier, the general public, and as a role model for the young. He went on USO tours after completing the season, visiting army hospitals and rehabilitation centers. He spoke with recovering GIs, many of whom were amputees, reassuring them that they too could beat the odds and lead a healthy, happy, and successful life after the war. In his attempt to fulfill all of these responsibilities, Pete Gray touched the heart of the nation. One event, in particular, forced Gray to come to terms with himself as a role model for others.

While he was playing for Memphis, the Chicks' front office received a poignant letter from a man by the name of Nelson Gary of Van Nuys,

Gray poses with six-year-old Nelson Gary Jr. of Van Nuys, California, shortly after being promoted to the Browns in 1945. The youngster, who lost his arm in an automobile accident, adopted Pete as his hero during his days as a Memphis Chick. (Courtesy of Bettmann.)

California. His six-year-old son, Nelson Jr. had also lost his right arm in an automobile accident, and Gray had become the young boy's inspiration. Through a community effort, the boy was able to travel to Memphis to meet his hero. A meeting was arranged between the two in the office of club president Edward Barry. At the first sight of Gray, the little boy raced across the room and leaped onto his hero's lap. Before Pete could utter a word, his admirer wrapped his arm around him and gave him a kiss on the cheek. The two immediately established a close relationship.[10]

That night's game against Nashville was dedicated to Nelson Gary Jr., who donned a Memphis Chicks' uniform complete with his hero's number "14" on the back. Although the One-Armed Wonder promised "to do my best to hit a home run" for the youngster, the best he could manage was a triple, double, and two singles to pace the Chicks to a 7–6 victory. When he looked over to the box seat where his young admirer was, Gray saw him fast asleep in his mother's arms.[11]

Before the Garys returned to California, young Nelson posed for a picture with his hero, both of them wearing their Chicks uniforms. New York sportswriter Bob Considine called the scene "one of the most touching events in sports" since the July 4, 1939, Lou Gehrig Day at Yankee Stadium. According to Considine, "You could almost hear the young boy saying to himself 'Just like Pete,' as he posed there in the shadow of big fellow, with his tiny bat cocked menacingly and resplendent in his miniature Chick uniform."

Gray, who usually came across serious but kind to his young admirers, was also deeply moved by the experience. In young Nelson, he must have seen a little bit of himself as a boy chasing after a dream. As much as he might have tried to distance himself from the little boy, Gray displayed more feeling for him than for any other fan. It wasn't a publicity stunt. Gray had too much integrity for that. It was a feeling of empathy for what the young boy had been through and what he would have to endure as a one-armed youngster who simply wanted to be like every other kid. Never one to show much emotion, the Chicks' star outfielder displayed his compassion for the youngster by offering some gruff but fatherly advice. "If the kid falls down, don't pick him up," Pete told Nelson Sr. as the Garys prepared for their return trip. "Don't let him ever feel sorry for himself. That's the way my father treated me." When Pete extended his left hand to bid his young fan goodbye, Nelson ran past the outstretched arm, embraced his hero in a warm hug and whispered, "I love you, Pete." Gray had been won over by the innocence and compassion of a six-year-old boy. It was as much as he would ever open himself to anyone outside of his immediate family and childhood friends.[12]

Nineteen forty-three was only a preview of better things to come for Pete Gray. He returned to Pennsylvania's Wyoming Valley in the off-season to be with family and friends, and engage in an unusual workout regimen that would allow him to crack the big leagues. Each day Gray would rise early in the morning to do his "road work," usually a two to three mile run through Nanticoke. The afternoons were spent up at the

"Pines," an open area located on the hills surrounding Hanover and shaded by pine trees. Gray's older brother Whitey, an amateur boxer, used the area as a training site and had set up gymnastic rings, a pull-up bar, and even a boxing ring. Pete used the rings and pull-up bar to strengthen his left arm and he would spar with his brother to develop better balance and agility on the basepaths. Often these workouts were followed by batting practice, usually one hundred swings a day. And if no one was around to pitch, Pete would simply take a walk along the railroad tracks with a broom handle, tossing pieces of gravel into the air and driving them left, right, and center.[13] The entire workout was unorthodox, but it would be difficult to deny its effectiveness.

In 1944, the Memphis Chicks and their star outfielder hit their stride together. As Gray went, so went the Chicks. He hit for average and for power, leading the club to a first place finish during the first half of the split season. The clincher came on June 6 in a game against the Chattanooga Lookouts at Engel Stadium. With the score tied at three apiece in the eighth, Gray came to bat against hurler Bob Albertson, the ace of the Lookout staff. Gray took the first two pitches outside and hit the next one, a fastball waist high and just inside, over a 20-foot fence that was 330 feet away from home plate. It proved to be the winning run in a game that clinched a first place finish for the Chicks in the first half of the split season. By then, Gray had compiled a .348 average with 5 doubles and 5 triples. He also led the league in stolen bases with 15.[14]

But the home run was something special for him. It was the first of five Gray would hit in his professional career, and all of them came during the '44 season. The second came three weeks later against Nashville, and the other three were inside-the-park jobs that were hit over the course of late August and early September while the Chicks were in the heat of the pennant race.[15] To be certain, Gray had the bat speed to hit a ball hard, but with one arm he simply did not have the power to hit home runs regularly. These days Gray claims that his only regret about his professional career is that he didn't try to hit more round-trippers. In fact, the secret to his success was his speed and his ability to play within his physical limits.

"I was fast all right, plenty fast," Gray admitted. "I never ran track in school, but I worked very hard on my own at stealing bases. It was one of the most important areas of the game for me." Gray claims that being sidelined by injuries prevented him from stealing more bases in his minor league career. "I had five stolen bases my first year in pro ball

After losing to Nashville in the first round of the Dixie League playoffs, Memphis finished the season in third place with an 85–55 record. It was a complete reversal of the '43 campaign in which the club posted a 56–81 record and finished last in the league. The difference was a healthy Pete Gray. The star outfielder is pictured in the top row, the first player on the left. (Courtesy of The Sporting News.*)*

at Three Rivers. Had I not broken my collarbone, I would have been closer to 30. Without a doubt, the 68 I stole in 1944 with Memphis was a much better indication of my ability."[16] Clearly it was Gray's ability to steal bases that caught the eye of big league scouts.

In late July Gray put on a base-stealing exhibition, pilfering nine bases in a five-game series against Birmingham. He swiped four during a Friday doubleheader, including two thefts of third, stole another the next day, and purloined another four during the Sunday doubleheader. By August 4th Gray had accumulated a total of 47 thefts and had a regular following of scouts watching him from the bleachers, including Bob Quinn of the Boston Braves, Bill Terry of the New York Giants, Hank Severeid of the Boston Red Sox, Harry O'Daniel of the Philadelphia Phillies, and Wish Egan of the Detroit Tigers. A week later in a game against Little Rock, Gray boosted his total to 58 by stealing four bases and eclipsing the all-time Chicks' mark of 54 set by Dixie Carroll in 1920.[17] After the game, Tigers scout Wish Egan phoned Detroit and recommended that the Tigers purchase Gray's contract from Memphis.

"We had a pretty slow club," said Egan, "and if the Tigers had Gray on the bench to do some pinch running in '44, we might have nosed the Browns out for the flag. As it turned out, the club had little interest in Gray and we lost quite a few runs in the last weeks of the season by having men thrown out trying to take an extra base in the clutch."[18] The St. Louis Browns, on the other hand, had more confidence in Gray's abilities.

Brownie scouts had been following Gray since the beginning of July, but it wasn't until the last home series against Mobile that they expressed their interest in the One-Armed Wonder. Gray didn't disappoint them either, finishing the homestand in a blaze of glory. In the first two games of the three-game series, he sparked Memphis to a pair of victories, going five for seven at the plate and stealing a couple of bases including a head-first theft of home. In the field he handled his seven chances perfectly. The next day, during the third and final game of the series, Gray collected his fifth home run, along with two doubles and a single to account for seven of the Chicks' eleven runs. The victory placed Memphis in a three-way tie for first place with Atlanta and Nashville.[19] After that game, the St. Louis scout Jack Fournier immediately wired Donald Barnes, the owner of the Browns: "War or no war, Gray is a big leaguer. Advise you to buy at once."[20]

The deal wasn't completed until September 29 when the Browns purchased Gray's contract from Memphis for $20,000, the largest sum of money spent on a Southern Association player to that date.[21] Unfortunately, by late September, the Chicks had lost their bid to capture the Southern Association title, losing to Nashville in the first round of the playoffs. The team finished its season in third place with an 84–55 record but found some consolation in the achievement of its star outfielder.

Gray was voted the Most Valuable Player of the Southern Association by the sportswriters who covered the circuit. It wasn't a sympathy vote either. Gray earned the award—his numbers were prodigious. In 129 games, he compiled a .333 average while collecting 119 hits for 221 total bases and drove in 60 runs. His .996 fielding percentage and 336 put-outs led all Southern Association outfielders and his 68 stolen bases tied a league record set in 1925 by a future Hall-of-Famer, Hazen "Kiki" Cuyler, who starred for the Cubs and Pirates.[22] Those were big league statistics for *any* player, but for a one-armed player they were an unbelievable achievement. Pete Gray had beaten the odds once again, and this time he won big time.

*Gray meets with Brownies Zack Taylor, Fred Hofmann, and Charles DeWitt
shortly after signing his major league contract. (Courtesy of* The Sporting News.*)*

When *The Sporting News* presented him with the MVP award in
mid–September, Gray went on public record with a brief, modest statement: "This award is by far the greatest thrill of my playing career. Thank
you." But he admitted, years later, that the only thought running through
his mind at the time was: "I can play with those fellas in the majors, and
I'd like to have the chance to show 'em what I can do!"[23] The next season
he would have that chance. For now though, it was time to celebrate and
to enjoy his success.

In December, after completing another USO tour, Gray returned to
Pennsylvania's Wyoming Valley and was honored at a testimonial dinner
in Wilkes-Barre. More than five hundred guests attended, including Edward Barry, president of the Chicks, Doc Prothro, the Memphis manager, Earle Mack, son of legendary manager Connie Mack of the Philadelphia Athletics, Chief Albert Bender, once the star of the Athletics'
pitching staff, Jimmy Foxx of the Chicago Cubs, and Manager Richard
T. Porter and General Manager Michael J. McNally of the Wilkes-Barre
Barons.

It was a personal victory for Gray. Some of the very same people who refused to give him an opportunity to play professional baseball only two years earlier had now gathered to honor him and his remarkable achievements with the Memphis Chicks. The most heartfelt tribute came from Edward Barry, president of the Chicks, who said, "Two of the greatest thrills of my life were produced by Pete Gray in the past season. The first was a home run that put our ball club into the lead in the Southern Association and the second was the visit of Nelson Gary. When I saw that little boy enter my office and jump into his hero's lap, I knew we had something special in Pete Gray." Barry concluded by pledging the Chicks' continued support of Gray, promising that "when the St. Louis Browns play their first home game in 1945, one thousand Memphians will be in the stands to let Pete know that we will never forget him. That's how our great city feels about the man voted the most courageous player in baseball."[24]

The tribute touched Gray deeply. As he stood to speak, the one-armed outfielder found it difficult to restrain his emotions. The gathering tried to help him out by giving their hometown hero a standing ovation. When it was over, Gray thanked everyone for their support, especially Edward Barry and Doc Prothro for "giving me a chance, and for the two best years of my entire baseball career."[25]

Pete Gray had beaten the odds that relegated most everyone else in the Wyoming Valley to a life in the coal pits. He had become a "somebody." Now it was time for him to move up to the majors. Time to realize his life-long dream.

Last in the American
League . . . Until 1944

"The only time I ever felt pity for a major league ball club was when I visited Sportsman's Park to watch the Browns."—
Anonymous sportswriter

W ORLD WAR II may have depleted the ranks of quality players from the major leagues, but it was certainly good to St.
Louis baseball. By 1942, Branch Rickey, the general manager of the National League Cardinals, built a team that would capture
three successive pennants. That team featured twenty-game winners
Mort Cooper and Johnny Beazley and the incredible outfield trio of Enos
Slaughter, Terry Moore, and Stan Musial. In the 1942 World Series, the
Cardinals upset the heavily favored Yankees four games to one to win
the first of their two wartime championships. The second came in '44
against their city rivals, the Browns.[1]

Until 1944, it seemed as if the only thing the St. Louis Browns had in common with their extremely successful National League counterpart was a stadium, Sportsman's Park. Both clubs shared the park located on the north side of the city, playing there when the other was on a road trip. If the Cards were the pride and joy of St. Louis baseball, the American League Browns had been the city's laughingstocks, perennial losers plagued by nearly a half-century of frustration and futility on the diamond.

In 1902, the Browns relocated to St. Louis from Milwaukee. They became part of the upstart American League which competed for player talent and fan loyalty with the more established teams of the National League. Not surprisingly, the first Brownie owner, Robert Hedges, lured seven Cardinals to his team in the franchise's inaugural year. When the '02 campaign began, the Cards countered by seeking a court injunction against the American League club for playing seven of *their* men. While the luring of National League players allowed the Browns to capture a second place finish in that first year, it also instigated a strong rivalry between the two clubs that would exist until 1953 when the Browns left town.

After their initial success of 1902, the Browns went on to finish in the second division 32 times in the next 40 seasons. They finished dead last on seven occasions, the worst season coming in 1939 when the team compiled a season record of 43–111 for a .279 winning percentage. If it had not been for Philadelphia and Boston, which suffered periodic dry spells and nosed out the Brownies for last place during eight other seasons, St. Louis would have held a monopoly on the American League basement during this forty year period. But even Browns fans—who established a rather self-deprecating "cult of losers"—had their moments of glory.

What Brownie loyalist could forget the 1922 season, when St. Louis finished second to the Yankees and won a club record 93 games? That '22 team led the American League in seven categories: team batting average (.313); team slugging percentage (.455); triples (94); stolen bases (132); most strikeouts compiled by a pitching staff (534); fewest walks (421); and lowest earned run average (3.38). There would also be third-place finishes in 1921, '25, '28, and '42, thanks to such star players as the classy first baseman and future Hall-of-Famer George Sisler, outfielder Ken Williams, who hit more home runs than Babe Ruth in 1922 with 39, and pitcher Urban Shocker, who won at least 20 games a season for the Browns between 1920 and 1923.[2]

Nevertheless, there was something tragically comic about the Browns' successes. In 1938, for example, pitcher Louis Norman Newsom, more affectionally known as "Bobo" by the Brownie fans, was on his way to posting 20 wins and capturing the American League strikeout crown for a team that would finish seventh. Going into the last game of the season, Bobo led Bob Feller of the Cleveland Indians by two strikeouts, with both hurlers scheduled to make one final start. Newsom rose to the occasion, fanning 13 to cap a 5–1 win over the Philadelphia Athletics. When Bobo discovered that the Indians had lost their game to the Tigers, 4–1, he assumed that he had clinched the strikeout title. When he reached the clubhouse he immediately phoned Detroit and got Feller on the line.

"I just wanted to give you a chance to congratulate the AL's new strikeout king," boasted Newsom, "because I whiffed thirteen in getting my twentieth win today." Feller laughed and replied, "Congratulations on number twenty, Bobo, but I've got some bad news for you on that other score. Even though I lost here, I set a new AL strikeout record with eighteen, so I'm afraid it's you who will have to congratulate me!" After a long pause, the Brownie hurler finally broke the silence with the jibe, "Well, I hope it still ain't too late to make this call collect!"[3]

The Browns' fans came to appreciate the irony of mixed success that seemed to characterize the club's ownership. Several owners were also local brew kings who enjoyed more success with beer than with baseball. Budweiser, Falstaff, and Alpen Brau were all products of their personal enterprise and were advertised on the outfield walls and scoreboard at Sportsman's Park. This mixed success was not lost on the Brownie fans, who quipped that their team was "first in booze and last in the American League."[4]

Despite their colorful history, the St. Louis Browns would finally gain some respectability during the war years. World War II seemed to transform the very nature of the club from a conglomeration of lackluster performers into a team of scrappy, die-hard ballplayers. According to Manager Luke Sewell, the Browns were "representative of the war years themselves, combative and highly competitive." Sewell attributed their aggressiveness to the "frustrations resulting from an uncertain future" in professional baseball, which resulted in a "great deal of intestinal fortitude among the players."[5]

Military service had taken its toll on the Browns, as it did on every team in major league baseball. But in 1944 a peculiar combination of luck, raw determination, and even some talent allowed the Browns to lift

the proverbial monkey off their backs and capture their first and only
pennant. The team was composed of Cardinal castoffs such as Nelson
Potter, a veteran right-hander who might have compiled 20 wins for the
club had he not been suspended for allegedly throwing a spitball. Others
who found a home with the Browns after their Cardinal days were Don
Gutteridge, a pepperpot second baseman who on June 30 took part in
five double plays in one game, setting a since-surpassed AL second baseman's record, and outfielder Gene Moore, who solidified the Browns'
defense in '44 by coming off the bench and making some fine plays in
right field during the pennant race. To be sure, the Browns also possessed some bona fide big league talent that season.

George McQuinn, Mark Christman, and Vern Stephens had not yet
reached the peak of their careers by '44 and, indeed, made their reputation with the St. Louis Browns. McQuinn was a solid-hitting, picture-
perfect first baseman who had spent seven years in the Yankee farm
system while Lou Gehrig reigned in New York. He was finally drafted
by the Browns in 1938, and the next season, put together a 34-game hitting streak, finishing the season with a .324 average. McQuinn remained
a Browns' regular for eight years, leading AL first basemen in fielding
three times and in assists twice. Christman was a much lighter hitter than
McQuinn, but his steady fielding attracted the Browns, who purchased
him from the Detroit Tigers organization. In 1944, his first year as the
Brownie third baseman, Christman led AL third sackers with a .972
fielding average and knocked in a career-high 83 RBIs. His teammate
on the left side of the infield, Vern Stephens, signed with the Browns for
a $500 bonus at age 17. Four years later he had established himself as
the best homer-hitting shortstop in the game. In '44, Stephens led the
AL in RBIs and finished third in the MVP voting behind Tiger pitcher
Hal Newhouser.[6]

All of these players had been classified 4-F by their local draft
boards, plagued by bad backs, trick knees, or flat feet. Despite their
disabilities, which did on occasion hamper their ability to perform on the
diamond, these Brownies played each game during the '44 campaign as
if it were their last. It very well might have been for the teenagers, graybeards, or 4-Fs who found themselves filling in as temporary replace-
ments for the major leaguers who were serving in Europe or the Pacific.
That is why the '44 Browns played with a "don't give a damn" attitude,
never apologizing for their abandon in the field or on the basepaths. But
capturing a pennant was the furthest thing from their minds.[7]

"I don't think any of us who had been with the Browns for a number of years ever gave a thought to winning the pennant in '44," said McQuinn. "Oh, no. We were the St. Louis Browns and had *never* done anything like that before. Why would '44 be any different?"[8] Don Gutteridge agreed: "The trouble with the Browns was that the team was plagued with a defeatist attitude. Sure, we played hard and had some pretty good ballplayers, but we didn't think we could ever win a pennant. That kind of defeatist attitude was eating up the Browns, year after year."[9] Even Manager Luke Sewell was about as optimistic as the St. Louis sportswriters who had written off the Browns for another last place finish. "I thought just like anyone else, that we'd be lucky to get through the year," he admitted. "It was a makeshift club. Quite a few of the players were marginal from a major league standpoint."[10] To his credit though, Sewell was an outstanding manager able to get the most out of his players. His expert handling of a solid pitching staff kept the Browns in the chase through September, despite their .252 team batting average— one of the lowest in the American League.

Sewell's playing career as a catcher for the Cleveland Indians, Washington Senators, and Chicago White Sox prepared him well for the managerial post of such a team. Never a great hitter, Sewell compiled a lifetime batting average of .259 but he was dependable in the clutch, able to drive in the tying or go-ahead run when his team needed it most. However he was better known for his defensive prowess, setting a since-broken AL record by leading league catchers in assists four years (1926–28 and 1936) and another AL record of 20 seasons as an active catcher. Sewell was also able to keep his team in contention with his expert handling of marginal pitching staffs wherever he played.[11]

When he became manager of the Browns in 1941, Luke Sewell inherited a team that would learn from his experience, confidence, and perseverance. His philosophy was simple: "I want my ballplayers to do what they can do best. If they can improve on that and not try something which they can't do, then I'll be happy." This did not mean that Sewell discouraged needed work in other facets of the game, simply that he wanted his players to "stick to their strong points" and be creative enough to refine them. In those areas that needed work, they would do well to play "standardized baseball, sticking to a more uniform pattern."[12] The '44 Browns listened and learned.

One of the main features of the Browns that season was the marvelous defensive play of an infield consisting of McQuinn on first, Gutteridge at second, Stephens at short, and Christman at third, and a platooned outfield of Chet Laabs, Mike Kreevich, Milt Byrnes, Al Zarilla, and Gene Moore. Together with the pitching of Potter, Jack Kramer, Bob Muncrief, Sig Jakucki, and Denny Galehouse, the Browns' defense allowed the club to jump off to a sudden start, winning the first nine games of the campaign. It was so sudden, in fact, that the experts considered it a fluke. Key pitching and remarkable defensive support kept the Browns in a four-team dogfight with Boston, Detroit, and New York through most of the season.

In late September, the race narrowed to three contenders. Boston could not sustain itself after losing ace pitcher Tex Hughson and star second baseman Bobby Doerr to the war and dropped out of the race. On September 27 Detroit moved one game ahead of the Browns and three ahead of the Yankees. Two days later the stage was set for a dramatic finish as the Yankees went to St. Louis for a doubleheader, while Detroit hooked up with Washington for two games.

After the Browns came from behind to take the opener, Potter pitched a brilliant six-hit, 1–0 shutout in nightcap. The Brownies managed to win that second game on only two hits and a miracle over-the-shoulder catch by center fielder Mike Kreevich in the eighth inning with two Yankee runners aboard. Detroit split its twin bill with Washington, and both the Tigers and Browns entered the final two days of the season with the identical 87–65 records. The two contenders stayed even on September 30, as the Browns blanked the Yankees 2–0 behind the brilliant pitching of Denny Galehouse, while Detroit's Hal Newhouser captured his 29th victory over the Senators. That brought the race down to the final day of the '44 season.[13]

On Sunday, October 1, 37,000 fans packed St. Louis' Sportsman's Park to root for the Brown and Orange. The scene was set for high drama as the Browns gave the call to Sig Jakucki, who was looking for his 13th victory of the season. If the Browns won, they stood to clinch at least a tie for the AL flag, and with a Washington victory over Detroit they could capture the flag outright, putting an end to a string of unfortunate seasons that had haunted them more than any other team in major league baseball history. Not surprisingly, the game had an inauspicious beginning for St. Louis.

The Browns were trailing New York, 2–0, in the fourth inning without a hit off Yankee starter Mel Queen when Mike Kreevich got things started with a single and Chet Laabs followed with a homer. The game was tied at two apiece. An inning later, Kreevich came to bat with two outs and again singled. He was followed by Laabs, who hit a 3–1 pitch into the bleachers for another round tripper, giving the Brownies a 4–2 lead. Laabs, who during the season batted only .234 as a part-time player and had just three home runs to his credit before that day, had become an instant hero. During the seventh inning, the left field scoreboard informed the fans that Washington had defeated the Tigers by a 4–1 margin and an eerie silence fell over the stadium. The Browns now controlled their own destiny.

In the eighth, Vern Stephens' solo homer gave the Browns a 5–2 lead and an inning later, a pennant clinching victory. Not only had the Browns completed a four-game sweep of the New York Yankees, but in the process, they had become the "Cinderella Champions of the American League."[14] Amidst all the tears, laughter, and sheer jubilation of the Brownie faithful, the trollies stopped, the city stopped, and for a moment even World War II had stopped. The miracle had happened.

The Browns had captured the pennant with a record of 89 wins and 65 losses. Their winning percentage of .578 set a new low in American League history.[15] The St. Louis Cardinals, on the other hand, had clinched their third consecutive pennant in the most one-sided race in the National League in forty years. The Cards had won 73 of their first 100 games and finished the season with a 105-49 record, 14½ games over second-place Pittsburgh. In so doing, they became the first NL team to win over 100 games three years in a row. As a team, the Cardinals were an offensive powerhouse, leading the league in hits, runs, batting average, doubles, and home runs. Stan Musial hit .347, Johnny Hopp .336, and catcher Walker Cooper .317. The Cards could also boast of a strong pitching staff that led the league in strikeouts, shutouts, and earned-run average. The National League's three top pitchers in winning percentage were Redbird hurlers: Ted Wilks, who posted a 17–4 record for a winning percentage of .810; Harry Brecheen who went 16–5 and posted a .762 winning percentage; and Mort Cooper, the ace of the staff, who compiled a 22–7 record for a .759 victory percentage. The Cards' superb defense, anchored by shortstop and league MVP Marty Marion, established an all-time record for fewest errors with 112.[16] Together with the solid pitching and potent offense, their remarkable defensive play made the Cardinals untouchable. Not only were the Redbirds better than the Browns, they were also more experienced. Despite the age and journey man background of many Brownies, not one had ever appeared

in a World Series. That is why the St. Louis bookies quoted the Cards
at one to two and the Browns at eight to five.[17]

The 1944 World Series, more commonly known as the "Streetcar
Series," was played at Sportsman's Park and proved to be a pitchers'
series. Cardinal pitchers struck out 49 hitters while the Browns' hurlers
struck out 43. Their combined total of 92 strikeouts set a World Series
record that still stands today.

The Series opened on October 4 with a great pitching duel. Cardinal
pitcher Mort Cooper was scheduled to face Denny Galehouse, who had
compiled a 9–10 record over the course of the regular season but proved
to be the Browns' most effective pitcher down the stretch. Cooper surrendered only two hits to the Browns but was bested by Galehouse, who
scattered seven Redbird hits, and the Browns eked out a 2–1 win for
their first-ever World Series victory.

The Cardinals tied the Series the next day in an 11-inning battle before
35,000 fans. The Cards gave their hurler Max Lanier a two-run lead
through four innings, but the Browns tied the game in the seventh on Gene
Moore's single, a long double by Red Hayworth, and another base hit by
Frank Mancuso. The score remained deadlocked until the 11th when the
Cards' Ken O'Dea smashed a single to left that scored Ray Sanders from
second base, and the Cards won game two by a 3–2 margin.

On October 6 the Browns were vindicated with a 6–2 victory on the
strong pitching of Jack Kramer. George McQuinn proved to be the
catalyst of the Brownie attack, knocking out three hits for a total of three
runs. He was by far the best hitter in the series for either team, compiling
a terrific .438 average. In game four, the Cardinals touched Sig Jakucki
for two runs in the first on a Stan Musial home run and for two more in
the third on a single by the Cardinal outfielder. Although the Browns collected nine hits off Harry Brecheen, they managed to score only a single
run. Their best opportunity came in the eighth inning when, with one out,
Moore walked, Stephens singled him to third, and Laabs grounded hard
through the box toward centerfield. But Cards shortshop Marty Marion
managed to field the ball and shovel it to second base to start an inning-
ending double play. It was that kind of superior defense that kept the
Browns from generating many runs in the Series.

Despite a brilliant three-hit, ten-strikeout performance by Denny
Galehouse in game five, the Browns again came up empty-handed, losing
2–0. The Cards went up in the Series three games to two. Still, the
Browns refused to die.

Mike Kreevich was the only Browns' regular to hit over .300 in 1944. He would be waived to Washington the following season to make room in the Brownie outfield for Pete Gray. (Courtesy of Allied Photocolor.)

Behind the pitching of Nelson Potter and the hitting of George McQuinn, the AL pennant winners tried to battle back in game six. In the second, Laabs tripled to center and McQuinn singled him home for a 1–0 Brownie lead. Potter turned back all Cardinal hitters until the fourth when, with one out, he walked Cooper and gave up a base hit to Sanders. Cooper advanced to third on the hit. Cardinal third baseman Whitey Kurowski came to the plate and grounded a 2–2 fastball to Stephens at short. The Browns appeared to escape from the inning on an apparent double play ball – Stephens to Gutteridge to McQuinn – but both runners were called safe. Gutteridge had failed to touch the bag at second and Kurowski had beaten the throw to first. Cooper scored on the play. Verban and Lanier followed with base hits, driving in Sanders and Kurowski. The Cards won the game, 3–1, and the Series, 4–2.[18]

To be sure, the Browns had taken advantage of the military draft. They won the American League pennant with a team that included 13 players who were classified as "4-F," more than any other team had on its roster. The ability clearly existed to capture a pennant in the war-depleted majors: Mike Kreevich, the only regular to hit over .300; Vern Stephens, who hit .293 and led the AL in RBIs with 109; Mark Christman, who hit .271 and drove in 83 RBIs; and pitchers Nelson Potter (19–7), Jack Kramer (17–13), Sig Jakucki (13–9), and Denny Galehouse (9–10).

"People make a big deal about '44 being a war year and how our team benefited from all the 4'Fs," explained Nelson Potter when asked about the Browns' only pennant. "Well, look at the Cardinal players we played against in the World Series. Stan Musial, Whitey Kurowski, Max Lanier, Marty Marion, and Mort Cooper. No one ever talks about how they benefited from the war."[19] Potter has a point.

What always seems to get lost in any discussion of the '44 Browns is the character of the players on that team. They were scrappy, competitive ball players who simply refused to give up. How else could a club with a winning percentage of .578—one of the lowest for a pennant winner in major league history—manage to defeat the powerhouse Cardinals two times during the World Series and play competitively enough to prevent blowouts in their four losses? Cardinal shortstop Marty Marion gave them a lot of credit: "We thought we were going to just walk through them. Who in hell's the Browns, you know. By the time we got in that first game, we found out they were a pretty good ball club. Yes sir, we had a hell of a time beating those boys. They were tough. If they'd have beat us that second game, we'd have probably been in trouble. They certainly had a lot of pride, those Browns. They were a team that just wouldn't quit."[20] Neither would Pete Gray, who was about to join them. The fit looked to be perfect, or so it seemed in September of 1944 when the Browns purchased the contract of this One-Armed Wonder.

Living the Dream as
a St. Louis Brown

"As a kid growing up in Hanover, all I ever dreamed about was making the big leagues and playing in Yankee Stadium."–
Pete Gray

D ESPITE THE SUCCESS the Browns experienced in 1944, the franchise was not prospering at the gate. For the most part, St. Louis fans remained Cardinal fans. Owner Donald Barnes needed to find a way to win over the fans if he hoped to compete financially with the Cardinals during the '45 season. The Browns signed Pete Gray, in part, to help them meet their financial needs. A one-armed outfielder would draw crowds in any major league park, especially if he could play. Of course, the Browns denied any part of a publicity stunt.

"We're not signing Gray for publicity reasons," insisted Barnes. "Such baseball men as Billy Evans [president of the Southern Associa-

Browns' owner Donald Barnes insisted that Gray was "not signed for publicity reasons," but later handed his one-armed outfielder a $100 bonus when he discovered Gray's fan appeal in New York. (Courtesy of Allied Photocolor.)

tion] and Kiki Cuyler [Hall of Fame outfielder who played with Chicago, Pittsburgh, Brooklyn and Cincinnati] vow that Gray is the best prospect in the minors. We paid $20,000 for Gray and we're certainly not investing that kind of money in a player who can't make the team."[1] Charlie DeWitt, the club's traveling secretary, was just as adamant about Gray's talent. In late November, shortly after Gray's signing, DeWitt was approached by a St. Louis sportswriter who remarked. "I guess you're going to show Gray once around the circuit, get your money back and then

ship him to Toledo [the top minor league club in the Browns organiza-
tion]." Infuriated by the question, DeWitt exploded: "What the hell ever
gave you that idea? You are like a lot of other guys who don't know and
don't try to find out that Gray is a real ballplayer. He's fast, he knows
how to get the jump, and he was all by himself in base stealing in the
Southern Association. Aside from his speed, the guy is a good fielder,
and a fairly good hitter." DeWitt even stated that had the Browns purchased Gray's contract a year earlier, they might have had an easier time
capturing the AL flag. "If I told you that we almost lost the pennant
because we didn't have Pete Gray last fall, you'd probably laugh," he
snapped. "But I do remember the final game of the series against the
Athletics, when we sent Tex Shirley, a pitcher, in to run—and Tex fell
flat on his face ten feet from home plate with the tying run. If the
Philadelphia catcher hadn't let the ball get away from him, we would
have lost, dropped two games behind the Tigers, and never caught up."
After calming down a bit, DeWitt assured the scribe that Gray's signing
was certainly not a publicity stunt. "Take my word," he added, "Pete
Gray is going to make the major league grade on ability—not on sympathy, or as some sort of a front window showpiece. And if he can't make
the grade, he'll be the first one to ask to be sent away."[2]

Although DeWitt was telling a half-truth as far as the Browns' inten-
tions for Gray were concerned, he was correct in his assumption about
the outfielder's integrity. If Gray could not "make the grade" in the majors, he certainly would be the first to ask for his release. That was the
way he was raised by his immigrant parents, coal miners who believed
in a good day's work for a good day's pay. If nothing else, the anthracite
culture instilled in all of its young the belief that if you didn't earn the
job, you surely didn't deserve to keep it. Barnes tried to assure Gray that
he was signed for his abilities by writing a clause into his contract, em-
phasizing that the one-armed outfielder would not be exploited as a freak
or a curiosity. He also ordered Manager Luke Sewell to treat Gray as he
would any other ballplayer, to view him on his merits. And from the start,
Sewell obliged.

At the Browns' spring training camp in Cape Girardeau, Missouri,
Sewell made it clear that he was not going to give Gray any special treatment. He still had the starting line-up of his 1944 pennant-winning team,
and he believed that it was strong enough to repeat in '45. If Gray could
contribute to the team's success, Sewell would find a place for him in the
line-up, and he said as much to the press. "Pete Gray is just another

ballplayer to me," said the Brownie pilot. "I'll promise him every opportunity to make the grade, but he will have to stand or fall on what he
shows. We can't play him if he weakens the team."[3]

But Sewell wasn't naïve. He realized that the Browns' fiscal health
was tied to Gray and that there would be pressure from the front office
to play him. Therefore, he was careful to sing the praises of the one-
armed outfielder whenever the press asked for his opinion. "It is, of
course, too early to say what my opening line-up will be," Sewell told the
reporters. "But I will admit that Gray has surprised me with his power
and his splendid timing at bat after a winter's lay-off."[4] The manager
refused to make any binding statements about Gray's future with the
club, leaving open the possibility that he was indeed the "One-Armed
Wonder" everyone in the organization wanted to believe he was. So
Sewell left the press with a favorable evaluation of the rookie's talent: "He
surely gets a good piece of the ball, is unusually fast, and it is fascinating
to see what he can do with that one arm."[5]

If Sewell wasn't prepared to give any special favors to Gray, the one-
armed outfielder certainly didn't expect any. In fact, he seemed to win
over the support of his teammates and management early on. During his
initial batting practices, Gray began driving balls into the outfield as if
he had been playing all winter. He was just as impressive shagging fly
balls in the outfield, and younger fans soon flocked to imitate his one-
handed style. On one occasion, even Luke Sewell, in awe of Gray's
technique, picked up the outfielder's glove and tried to catch and throw
using just one hand. More important, while he simply wanted to be
judged on the merits of his ability, Gray understood the controversy surrounding his promotion and how it connected to the need for greater
receipts at the team's box office. Accordingly, he was careful not to
jeopardize his personal integrity or the goodwill of management in his
remarks to the press. When asked to make predictions about his performance in the big leagues, Gray responded diplomatically:

> I surely am going to give it everything I have. I want to make good, not
> only for myself, but for the Browns. I hope I can make a lot of money for
> them, for they are willing to give me my big chance. I know I've got to
> make good to be an attraction, but I do know thousands of people are
> rooting for me. I get letters and good wishes from fans all over the country.
> A lot of them come from servicemen. They'll be watching to see what I
> do in the box scores, and if I make the team, there will be a lot of them
> out to see me play.[6]

Portrait of a major leaguer (Courtesy of Allied Photocolor.)

Comments such as these demonstrated Gray's exemplary attitude. Together with his impressive practice performances in spring training, Gray's courteous treatment of the press endeared him to such sportswriters as Frederick Lieb. Lieb, who wrote for *The Sporting News*, was almost immediately impressed with the St. Louis rookie's all-consuming interest in baseball. In a March 22 article, Lieb wrote: "Pete Gray is a throwback to an era before ballplayers became interested in golf, bridge, aviation, and other sidelights. His one all-consuming desire is baseball and he is the type of player who eats, sleeps, dreams, and talks baseball."[7]

Lieb was especially charmed by Gray's apparent naïveté and his reserved but respectful attitude in fielding questions from the press. "Pete isn't loquacious; an interviewer has to draw him out," observed the baseball writer. "At times he gives a question considerable thought before replying. He freezes up if an interviewer is inclined to look upon him as a freak of curiosity. But when treated just as a ballplayer trying to make good, he melts and becomes more confidential." Lieb added that on those rare occasions, Gray displays a "pleasant, winning smile, which lights up an otherwise unexpressive face."[8]

The Sporting News demonstrated a keen interest in Gray throughout the spring of '45. As the baseball fans' most cherished weekly, it enjoyed a national as well as international circulation and thrived on stories that would appeal to the interests of American servicemen in particular. Additionally, it seemed as if everyone at home or abroad, baseball fan or not, was curious to see if Pete Gray could make the grade. It had a lot to do with the American fascination with courage and internal fortitude, qualities that were enthusiastically embraced by the wartime public— qualities that described the personal disposition of Pete Gray. *The Sporting News* was also interested in the Browns' chances for another pennant in '45.

The baseball weekly picked the Browns to repeat as AL champions in '45, "in spite of the fact that two young men named Newhouser and Trout are still with the Tigers who came home in '44 only one game behind Luke Sewell's entry." According to *The Sporting News*, the Browns would be "tougher to beat in '45" because they have "fine balance" and since they "have not lost a single player of any importance from last year's club with the exception of Denny Galehouse" who remained home to work in the war industry. The Tigers, on the other hand, were "vulnerable at the plate," weakened by the loss of Dick Wakefield to military service. At best they would finish third behind the Browns and the second-place Yankees of Joe McCarthy. Luke Sewell was a bit more cautious in his pre-season prediction.[9]

Sewell realized that with the loss of Galehouse, his pitching would not be as competitive as it was in '44. "It looks like another wide-open race," he claimed in March, "but I think we are still the club to beat." Sewell admitted that the Browns retained most of their pennant-winning team and were likely to have "more of a punch offensively with the addition of Babe Martin who can hit for distance and Pete Gray, who appears to be a real ball player."[10] For the first time ever perhaps, even the players

Manager Luke Sewell (seated in the first row directly above the bat boy) described the defending American League Champions as a "fairly representative bunch for the war years . . . combative and intensely competitive." Despite their aggressive nature, the '45 Browns could not reproduce their pennant winning ways and finished well behind the first place Detroit Tigers. Pete Gray is pictured in the top row, first player on the extreme left. (Courtesy of The Sporting News.*)*

felt good about their chances for another pennant coming into spring training. They were confident about their abilities and believed that if they could remain in the race through early September, the experience of the coaching staff would put them over the top. Pitcher Nelson Potter remembers those feelings well:

> That '45 club was just as good as the '44 pennant winner. Nearly everybody was back and Sewell was, of course, a fine manager. He knew and understood his players, he was a very good manipulator of the pitching staff, and an excellent tactician in game situations. Sewell also had two top coaches in Fred Hofmann and Zack Taylor, both of whom were highly respected by the players. With that kind of personnel, we all thought we could capture another flag."[11]

The Browns had reason to be optimistic. Compared to most of the other clubs in the American League, which were saddled with gray-beards and teenagers, the Brownies boasted an average player age of 30 years—young enough to possess the stamina and strength needed to be competitive in a close pennant race but also mature enough to have the major league experience sufficient to outsmart the opposition. Along

with the acquisition of Pete Gray, the competitiveness of the club prom-
ised to translate into bigger gate receipts too. Just in case it didn't, the
Browns' front office promoted the eight St. Louisans on the team (Coach
Fred Hofmann; catcher Joe Schultz; infielders Mark Christman and Len
Schulte; outfielders Milt Byrnes and Babe Martin; and pitchers Al Hol-
lingsworth and Al LaMacchia[12]). It was a team tailored to win over the
loyalties of the St. Louis baseball fans from the rival Cardinals. The
Browns would have their first opportunity to showcase that hometown
talent in the season's final exhibition games, the so-called "St. Louis City
Series" against the Cards.

On Saturday, April 7, before a crowd of 6,325, the Browns clinched
a 3–2 victory in the opener of the six-game series. That first game
featured the brilliant pitching of Sig Jakucki and the slugging of Len
Schulte and Vern Stephens. Schulte drove in the Browns' first run on a
double off the Cards' Blix Donnelly in the fourth inning amd homered
off Jack Creel in the seventh to tie the game at two apiece. Stephens'
round tripper in the eighth proved to be the winning margin. The Cards
came back with a 13–4 victory on Sunday to tie the series. Redbird
hurlers Mort Cooper and Ted Wilks held the Browns to just five hits, one
of them coming off the bat of Pete Gray in the eighth inning. Gray's first
hit against big league competition brought the crowd of 13,000 to their
feet, the beginning of a love affair between St. Louisans and the one-
armed rookie.

The City Series resumed on Tuesday, the 10th, with the Browns
outhitting, outfielding, and outrunning their National League rivals. While
the big Brownie bats were swung by McQuinn and Kreevich, both of
whom hit for the cycle, Gray's baserunning also figured in the attack.
After reaching first base on a walk in the eighth, Gray set up a decoy between first and second. With Gutteridge on third base, Gray purposely
got caught in a rundown, allowing his teammate to scamper home with
the final run of the game and a 7–2 victory. Rain halted game four of
the series after six innings, but the Browns still managed to cop a 10–3
decision. Cards' hurler Bud Byerly gave up two runs in the fourth inning
on a homer by McQuinn and two more in the fifth when Gutteridge
homered and Gray scored from second base on a Milt Byrnes single. For
the Browns, Potter yielded seven hits in his five innings of work, and a
circus catch by Gray helped the Browns seal the game in the sixth.

Jakucki got the call to pitch game five. Though he suffered through
some control problems early on, he proved to be unhittable. The Cards'

Outfielder Gray takes his defensive stance during a pregame practice session.
(Courtesy of Bettmann.)

three runs came off of two Brownie errors early in the game. Offensively, the Brownie attack erupted in the seventh after being held scoreless by Cards' pitcher Blix Donnelly for six innings. Babe Martin's seventh inning homer accounted for three runs, and the Sewell's men chalked up five more in the eighth. Gray went two for five and scored a run in the Browns' 8–3 victory. The Cards managed to salvage the final game, 2–1, on Sunday, April 1, but the Brownies had taken the series, four games to two, to retain their traditional dominance of the spring ritual.[13]

The St. Louis City Series was important for Gray, proving that he could successfully compete on the major league level. After a slow start in the first three games, in which Gray managed to collect only one scratch hit, the one-armed outfielder came alive. In his next seven at bats, Gray collected four hits—all singles—and drove in a pair of runs. He hit second in the order behind Gutteridge and was able to play hit-and-run ball so effectively that the .240 average he compiled for the six games was hardly an accurate measure of his offensive worth. Gray also played flawless defense in the outfield with 13 putouts and 1 assist, and his basestealing helped to ignite the Browns' offensive on at least three occasions.[14] Moreover, Gray seemed to have captured the hearts of the St. Louis fans.

Each time he stepped to the plate, Gray was given warm applause by the fans. In pregame practices Gray dazzled them with his remarkable fielding technique and endeared himself to them with his aggressive play during the contests. "They really wanted to see Pete succeed," recalled Brownie pitcher Al Hollingsworth, "and it wasn't that they were ignorant of the Browns' gimmick to use him as a drawing card in a war year. No, the St. Louis fans were too sharp for that."[15] Don Gutteridge learned early on that anyone who messed with Gray's performance, even if it was inadvertent, was subjected to the wrath of the fans. He recounted just such an incident early in the '45 campaign:

> Although I was a second baseman, there were those occasions when I was pressed into playing left field when Pete was in center. During this particular game, a ball was hit into left center and being unaccustomed to the position, I ran into Pete who was under the ball. I made him drop it, knocking him over in the process. The fans booed me pretty bad. Not surprisingly, the next day I was back at second base. Yeah, the fans were true blue for Pete Gray.[16]

Gray officially began his rookie season against the Detroit Tigers on opening day in St. Louis, April 17. Hitting second in the order and playing left field, Gray, in his first plate appearance, faced Hal Newhouser, who would go on to become a twenty-game winner that season, posting a 1.81 ERA and capturing the American League's Most Valuable Player award. Ironically, Newhouser, a southpaw, had been very successful during the previous season against the Browns, a team whose line-up was filled with right-handed hitters. But he knew nothing about the left-handed Gray. In their first encounter, Gray grounded to shortstop, but later in the game, he singled through the middle of the infield. Although the Browns won that first game, 7–1, they lost the other two games of the opening series with Detroit, 11–0 and 1–0. Worse, Vern Stephens, the hard-hitting shortstop who often served as the catalyst for the Brownie attack, severely jammed his left thumb and was out for the next five games, all of which the Browns dropped.[17]

When Stephens did return to the line-up on April 26 against Cleveland, he single-handedly won the game with a homer and a two-run single. Two days later, Stephens again led the Brownie attack in sweeping both ends of a double header, 3–2 and 6–4, against the Chicago White Sox. Still, the Browns' five-game losing streak had left them in sixth place with a winning percentage of .444.[18] Gray's status had also declined.

After his initial appearance against Detroit, the one-armed rookie went hitless in his next 13 at-bats and was removed from the starting line-up on April 29 in Chicago. Gray saw only sporadic playing time over the next three weeks as the Browns struggled to reach the .500 mark. Instead, Sewell went with Babe Martin and Milt Byrnes in left field at Cleveland, Detroit, and Washington.[19] The benching was difficult for Gray to accept. He had been a starter and nothing less than the star for every team he had played with in the minors and now, for the first time in his professional career, he was riding the hardwood. Gray began to question his own ability to play the game, wondering if in fact the Browns simply intended to exploit him as "a one-armed freak show" for the amusement of the fans.

Gray's roommate, pitcher Al Hollingsworth, did everything in his power to discourage those negative thoughts. "Pete was hard to get along with during the early part of that season," said the veteran southpaw. "Things weren't going so well for him at the plate and he had to be constantly reassured that he wasn't up in the majors because of a manpower shortage or publicity gimmick, but because they couldn't have kept him in the minors after his record in Memphis."[20]

Gutteridge also noticed Gray's dismal attitude. "He was kind of a loner," according to the Brownie second baseman, "who sometimes played cards in the clubhouse, but didn't communicate with us too much." Gutteridge wasn't sure if that was Gray's natural disposition or if he was allowing his recent misfortunes to get the best of him: "At first, I didn't think he wanted his teammates to like him, but over the course of the season I figured that he didn't really know how to handle his situation, that is, always wanting to be known as a ballplayer, not a *one-armed* ball player. He just didn't want to be exploited."[21]

Midway through May, Gray was hitting .180 and seeing little playing time. Sewell had been true to his word – he wasn't going to play the rookie if he couldn't help the club, even if the Brownie manager was being pressured by the front office to play him. It was no secret that Donald Barnes wanted to see Gray in the line-up. The Browns' owner constantly promoted Gray's abilities wherever the team traveled and attempted to keep his one-armed rookie content with periodic cash bonuses. Gray didn't know how to handle this treatment either:

> I remember our first trip to New York to play the Yankees. Barnes came up to me on the train and said with a big grin, "They're expecting a big crowd to see you tomorrow, over 70,000 people." Then he pulled out his wallet and gave me a $100 bill. How is that supposed to make you feel? Like you earned your pay for just showing up?[22]

The New York press was just as persistent. When criticized by the Big Apple's sportswriters for "misrepresenting" Gray and not playing him when all they had been writing about was the Browns' "One-Armed Wonder" in anticipation of his first appearance in Yankee Stadium, Sewell retorted: "I didn't misrepresent anything. You're the guys who did the misrepresenting. I didn't say Gray would be in the lineup today. If you had been watching the box scores, you would have known he wasn't in the lineup in the last two games at Boston. I'm not using Gray as a crowd puller when he isn't hitting."[23]

Sewell might not have used Gray as a "crowd-puller," but he certainly did attract the fans. In his Yankee Stadium debut, Friday May 18, the St. Louis rookie received a standing ovation from nearly seventy thousand for simply making a pregame appearance. Perhaps Sewell yielded to fan pressure the next day when he inserted Gray into the lineup. The one-armed rookie went two for five at the plate and played flawless defense in left field in the Browns' 4–2 victory. After losing the first two games of the series to the Browns, the Yankees did not draw as big a crowd for the Sunday doubleheader, but the 20,000 who attended Yankee Stadium on that day saw Pete Gray put on a performance they would never forget.[24]

Game one of the double bill got underway with Gray leading off against former 20-game winner Spud Chandler. After taking the first pitch, Gray lined a fastball into right field for the first hit of the game. Dur-

Gray's parents, Peter Sr. and Antoinette, visited their son as part of an entourage from Pennsylvania's Wyoming Valley which made a trip to Yankee Stadium during the '45 campaign. Playing in the "House That Ruth Built" was a childhood dream come true for the one-armed Brownie outfielder. (Courtesy of AP/Wide World Photos.)

ing his second trip to the plate, Chandler challenged Gray with another fastball on the first pitch. Once again, the Brownie outfielder hit a line drive single into right field. Chandler responded like a mad bull, kicking the mound in frustration. "He really couldn't handle the fact that I got a hit off of him," recalled Gray. "After all, who wants to give up a hit to a cripple, especially one who had the nerve to crowd the plate."[25] It would only get worse for Chandler. Gray would collect two more hits and two RBIs off the Yankee hurler that afternoon and pace the Browns to a 10–1 win in the opener.

In the second game Gray only collected one hit on a remarkably well executed hit-and-run. But in the field he was spectacular. He had six putouts, three of which were curving line drives caught just above the shoestrings on the dead run. The Browns took the second game, 5–2, and ended up sweeping their four-game series with the Yankees. The sweep raised the spirits of everyone on the team, placing them in a tie with Detroit for second place and only two games behind the league-leading White Sox.

For Gray, the series was something special. Not only did he realize his childhood dream of playing in Yankee Stadium, he did it so well that he regained a starting role in the Brownie outfield. Gray batted .333 in the New York series, raising his season average to .225. While all his hits were singles, he did display the power to drive in some runs and proved that he had a keen batting eye, rarely chasing a bad pitch or swinging without connection. He also played remarkably well in the outfield, handling nine rather difficult chances without error. Perhaps most important for Pete, he did it all in front of his family and friends who travelled from the Wyoming Valley to see their local boy make good.

One of the fondest memories Gray has of that '45 season with the Browns was a visit with his father and brother Tony in the visitors' locker room before his Yankee Stadium debut. Gray was apologetic as he knew that he was not slated to start in the Friday night game, and he felt badly that his family had travelled the long distance to see him warm the bench. But neither of the Wyshners would hear of an apology. Instead, Pete Sr. told his son, "It doesn't matter if you play or not. What matters is that you are here, that you made it. No matter how many times they closed the door in your face, you never quit. You made it. You *are* a somebody!" Tony Wyshner, who had taught his younger brother how to play the game as a young boy and who still trained with him in the off-season, echoed his father's praises. "This is it, Pete," he said. "This is what you've worked for all your life. You are living your dream and I couldn't be prouder of you." Years later, Pete Gray would confess that no other moment in his major league career meant as much to him as that locker room visit in Yankee Stadium.[26]

Gray's attitude seemed to change for the better after the New York series. If he had given in to self-pity before that time, he learned to overcome it quickly. He even seemed to rediscover his sense of humor in a Washington barber shop. Having gone there for a shave, Gray was repeatedly nicked on the chin by the barber. After the shave, Pete surveyed the damage in the mirror. "Say, did I ever work for you before?" asked the barber. "No," replied Pete. "I lost my arm when I was a kid."[27]

Gray also seemed to recapture his self-assurance for playing the game. The Browns had once again become a contender by June, and Gray was contributing to their success on a regular basis. In a game against Philadelphia, he went two for four, stole three bases, and knocked in two runs to help the Browns cop an 8–2 victory. After the game, Connie Mack, the legendary manager of the Athletics approached the one-armed rookie, offered his hand, and apologized for not taking him more seriously five years earlier when he requested a tryout. "Son," said Mack, "I was wrong about you and you certainly proved it here today!"[28] Gray had been vindicated. He would enjoy another personal victory a week later on June 10th in Cleveland, where 65,000 packed the Indians' stadium to see the One-Armed Wonder. He didn't disappoint them either.

In the opener, Gray hit second and played center field, going two for four and scoring the only Brownie run in a 2–1 defeat. In the second game, he paced the Browns to a 4–1 victory over the Indians' Allie Reynolds, going three for five with 2 RBIs.[29] The performance put to rest the cynicism of one of Gray's biggest critics, Cleveland sportswriter Ed McAuley, who had stated in previous columns that Gray was "nothing more than a gate attraction" and that Manager Luke Sewell had been "saddled" with the one-armed outfielder and was "far from happy about the set-up." The morning after the double header with Cleveland, McAuley admitted in print that Pete Gray did, indeed, belong in the big leagues:

> The Browns no longer can be suspected of hiring Gray for box office purposes. That he helps the gate is inevitable. But that he helps the Browns win games now is evident to all who have watched him play. More power to him.[30]

If Pete Gray was a crowd pleaser, it was because of his exceptional ability to make an extremely difficult manuever seem effortless, whether in the field or at the plate. His motion for catching the ball, exchanging it to his hand, and throwing it was so quick that all three stages were completed in the blink of an eye. In order to complete this task with the greatest speed, Gray removed almost all the padding from his glove, wearing it on his fingertips with the little finger purposely extended outside of the mitt. He was then able to catch the ball, place the glove under the stump of his right arm, roll the ball across his body with his left hand, and throw it into the infield.

Because of the rapidity with which the one-armed outfielder could

Gray demonstrates how he would throw the ball after making a catch by slipping his glove under the stump of his right arm, then letting the ball roll down into his left hand. (Courtesy of AP/Wide World Photos.)

execute this motion, it was difficult at times for the umpires to decide whether he held the ball long enough after he caught it to constitute a legitimate catch. American League President William Harridge reduced their burden when he instituted a rule that allowed for momentary possession and, after making a catch, if Gray dropped the ball while shedding his glove for a throw, the catch still stood.[31]

Although Gray was only 6 feet and 150 pounds, his left arm was so powerful that it could wield a 36-ounce bat, a bat heavier than that used by most two-armed hitters in the majors in the 1940s. He achieved better bat control than most hitters by holding the bat about three inches from the end of the handle and swinging like a buggy-whip golfer. Much of his power was generated from his quick left wrist and strong forearm which measured 11 inches, only an inch less than his bicep. Pitchers would try to take advantage of the one-armed rookie by blowing fastballs by him, but Gray had a superb eye and a keen sense of timing. Even though he had to begin his swing early to compensate for his handicap, these assets allowed him to excel as a fastball hitter. He also had exceptional speed, which permitted him to become a fine bunter. He beat out many of the bunts he set down on the third base side or past the pitcher for base hits.[32] Wherever he went, the fans applauded. Of course, his most loyal following watched him perform in St. Louis' Sportsman's Park.

For Browns fans, the One-Armed Wonder could do no wrong. Even if he struck out, the fans cheered for him. They demanded that he play, regardless of how he was batting. Many would call the box office to see if Sewell had written his name into the lineup before coming out to the park. And if he played someone else, Sewell became *persona non grata*.[33] This fierce loyalty towards Gray helped the Browns at the box office, too. By the beginning of June, the Browns had won over a substantial number of Cardinal fans. Although their winning percentage was lower than it had been the year before, nearly 150,000 more customers had attended Browns games by that date than had by that same point during the pennant-winning 1944 season.[34]

America's involvement in World War II also contributed substantially to Gray's popularity. For wounded veterans and their families, the one-armed outfielder became a heroic symbol on the homefront. Gray asked for no sympathy from anyone; rather he stepped up to the plate, holding his bat in his left hand—a picture of defiance—and competed with all rivals. His example gave the veterans hope that they too could succeed in whatever career they chose as long as they gave it their all.

Gray gives a hitting demonstration for amputees at Walter Reed Hospital, Washington, D.C. It was one of many visits he paid to army hospitals and rehabilitation centers during his seasons in Memphis and St. Louis. His great respect for American servicemen led him to downplay his own personal struggle to become a major league baseball player as he publicly stated that "there is no courage about me, courage belongs on the battlefield." (Courtesy of The Sporting News.*)*

Gray delivered this message on playing fields across the country. It seemed that American servicemen who returned home from the war as amputees were there at every ball park waiting for him, individuals such as Private Pat Gervace, who lost an arm in the Battle of Huertgen Forest. Gervace, who attended the doubleheader between the Browns and the Indians at Cleveland, asked to meet Gray and was taken to the visitors' locker room after the games. As awkward as Gray may have felt, he spent nearly an hour with the young veteran, assuring him that he had a productive future and autographing a baseball for him.[35] There were others, too.

During the Browns' road trip to Washington in late May, Gray visited a group of amputees at Walter Reed Army Hospital. There he was interviewed by Manager Luke Sewell over the public address system. Sewell asked his rookie questions ranging from how he lost his arm to how he broke into organized ball. The Brownie pilot concluded the interview with the statement: "So much fuss has been made over Pete Gray that he'd have to be as good as Babe Ruth to live up to what people expect of him. However, he is a fine player, fast, courageous, and he can hit. We use him when he can help us win, the same as any two-armed player." Sewell's message was candid as well as respectful of Gray and the other amputees, who wanted to be regarded like any other human being.

Following the interview, Gray gave an impressive demonstration of hitting and fielding. The informal exhibition received a tremendous ovation from the veterans and also inspired many questions as well as comments. One veteran suggested, for example, that if Gray would take a full basketball pivot and then get off his throw, he would generate more power. After trying the pivot several times, Gray seemed to be pleased with it. "Thanks, fella," replied the one-armed rookie. "That's something that hadn't occurred to me. I'm going to continue to work on that pivot in my fielding practices." Sewell underscored the importance of footwork for Gray, explaining that Pete's skilled fielding depended on "agile footwork" and that, "like a boxer, Pete is always in position to make the next move."[36]

The dialogue was inspirational as well as informative and deep down, Gray took something more than a new fielding technique away from the experience with him. It was a feeling of empathy for others. Just as he had inspired them, so too did they inspire Pete Gray.

Reversal of Fortune

"Even though Pete Gray was a miracle man in a lot of ways, he still couldn't do as good a job as a guy with two arms, let's face it. There's no question that he cost us quite a few ball games when we were trying to win a pennant." —George McQuinn, quoted in Teenagers, Graybeards, and 4-F's *(1982)*

P ETE GRAY'S PLAYING time diminished as the '45 campaign unfolded. His productive games became few and far between. By late June, he had appeared in a total of 32 games, and not all of them were in starting roles. On occasion, Gray filled in as a pinch hitter, runner, or fielder. Regardless of his role, Gray's 103 at-bats resulted in limited production: 23 hits—2 doubles, a triple, and 3 sacrifices—12 runs scored, and a .222 average. As his playing time lessened, so did his patience with the men in blue.

Gray became very argumentative at the plate. The umpires did not appreciate the one-armed rookie's bickering either. Gray put the umps in a vulnerable position, since the fans would immediately come to his defense whenever they saw him upset. It was an unusual situation. On one hand, the fans admired Gray for his success in competing on even terms, but on the other, they wouldn't allow him to be treated on even terms because of his handicap.

When asked how he felt about his status with the Browns, Gray told *The Sporting News's* Fred Lieb, "I don't think I've made good yet, especially when I have to sit on the bench while Luke Sewell plays Don Gutteridge, an infielder, in left field." Gray realized, however, that Sewell was trying to get more offensive punch in the line-up, and he even admitted that "so far, my hitting hasn't entitled me to a regular starting position." Still, Gray refused to concede that he had not earned the respect of the other AL clubs, who tended to play their outfielders in against him.

"It isn't the outfielders playing in for me that bothers me," said Gray. "It is the infielders playing me closer than any other hitter, always expecting a bunt." Moreover, the one-armed outfielder insisted that his recent performances at the plate demonstrated his ability to hit the long ball. "I really started hitting the ball for some distance when we last played in Cleveland and Detroit," he pointed out. "If the outfielders had played me close, I would have made a number of extra base hits. As it was, I did get my first major league extra base hits, a triple and a double. In Detroit, I missed my first homer by about six inches."

Gray also admitted that he had mixed emotions about his value to the club and its fans. "I wonder if the Browns regret that they purchased me," he said frankly, "though I know I have done them a lot of good at the gate." While Gray was "genuinely touched" by all the fan support he had received, he also wondered whether it was more from sympathy than from a genuine respect for his ability. "After all, if I couldn't make those catches, I wouldn't be out there," he said. "In fact, I never would have gotten my chance to play big league ball."[1]

Whether he wanted to admit it or not, though, it was inevitable for any one-armed player to have some natural vulnerabilities because of his handicap. It had only been a matter of time before opposing teams discovered them and exploited those weaknesses to their advantage, and Gray did have some weaknesses.

Had he been thrown nothing but fastballs, Pete Gray might have remained a .300 hitter at the major league level. Soon, however, opposing pitchers discovered that Gray could not hit the slower breaking balls.

Almost all of the 51 hits he collected that season were to center or left field off fastballs that were thrown on the outside half of the plate. Timing was the secret to Gray's success as a hitter. Once he started his swing he could not change his timing, and the fact that he had no second hand to check his swing made him extremely vulnerable to curve balls. Gray also had difficulty hitting low pitches or making contact with pitches that were thrown inside.[2] White Sox hurler Ed Lopat used that knowledge to his advantage whenever he faced the one-armed rookie. "I'd jam him with fastballs because he had trouble getting around on the inside pitches," he explained, "and when he'd open up his stance to compensate, I'd make him chase a pitch outside."[3] Lopat's manager, Jimmy Dykes, said that the league's other pitchers also took advantage of Gray's vulnerability at the plate. "He simply couldn't get the bat down fast enough to hit the low ones," according to Dykes. "When other pitchers around the league discovered this weakness they stopped trying to overpower him with fastballs and fed him a steady diet of breaking balls or pitches that were low and away," he added. "In the end, that's what ruined Pete Gray as a major league baseball player."[4] But Gray had other weaknesses too.

The St. Louis rookie experienced some difficulty in the outfield. Even though Gray was adept at removing the ball from his glove and throwing it, a one-armed player could not avoid giving runners a few additional seconds as he transferred the ball from his glove to the opposite hand for a throw. Runners would often try to take the extra base on Gray, and often they succeeded.[5]

Despite his vulnerabilities as a one-armed player, Gray managed to raise his average to .260 by mid–July. During a three-game homestand against the Philadelphia Athletics, the rookie went four for eight with two RBIs. His double in the ninth inning of the second game of a July 4th doubleheader drove in the tying and winning runs, giving the Browns a 6–5 victory and avoiding a loss of the twin bill.[6] He continued his hot hitting when Washington came to town, again going 4 for 8 with 2 RBIs in a three-game series. Gray's performance allowed the Browns to capture two victories from the Senators, 7–3 and 5–1, and return to the .500 mark.[7] Gray's successful homestand also resulted in a campaign by the sportswriters of the *St. Louis Post-Dispatch* to get the one-armed outfielder regular playing time.

"It really does seem that he improves with usage," wrote John E. Wray in his Wednesday, July 5 column after Gray went three for four against the Athletics the previous day. "Perhaps if he were kept in there regularly he might fully regain the hitting form that lifted him high in the Southern Association."[8]

Though also a big Gray fan, another *Post-Dispatch* writer, Roy Stockton, was a bit more objective about the rookie's situation:

> It is difficult for Gray to be "just another ball player" because his value at the box office has been all out of proportion to his ability as a ball player. Every day fans want to see him in action, so do many of the baseball scribes. But Pete isn't in there every day, either because his hitting doesn't warrant it, or because his physical condition will not allow him to perform.[9]

More insightful though, was Stockton's insight that Gray's sensitive disposition was beginning to irk his teammates, many of who had been envious of all the publicity their one-armed teammate was attracting:

> There is also a club problem about Pete Gray. Manager Sewell insists that Pete is just another ball player on the club and accepted as just that in the dugout and in the clubhouse. But while the players haven't confided in Luke about their personal feelings, there has been resentment here and there. Undoubtedly, Gray senses the resentment, slight though it may be, when with only one arm he is sometimes able to outhit and outfield players with two arms. Perhaps in reprisal, Pete bristles a bit."[10]

To be sure, many of the Brownies admired Gray for overcoming his handicap to play major league baseball, but as the season wore on into August and the Browns found themselves stuck in seventh place, 8½ games in back of the league-leading Tigers, some began to blame Gray for their dismal season. Mike Kreevich, who had played center field and hit .301 for the pennant-winning Browns the previous year, was personally insulted whenever he was platooned with Gray. "If I'm not playing well enough so a one-armed man can take my job, I should probably quit the big leagues," he often complained to his teammates.[11] However, before Kreevich could walk out, the Browns waived him.

Others were openly critical of Gray, resenting what they perceived to be management's decision to jeopardize a pennant for good public relations. George McQuinn was among the disillusioned players:

> Even though Pete Gray was a miracle man in a lot of ways, he still could not do as good a job as a guy with two arms. Let's face it. He couldn't field

Although Gray was adept at removing the ball from his glove and transferring it to his throwing hand, the process gave opposing baserunners an additional second or two to take the extra base. (Courtesy of Allied Photocolor.)

ground balls or flies or shift his glove quickly enough to get the ball back to the infield as fast as the average man. There's no question that he cost us quite a few ball games. I'll be frank with you and say we did get to resent Gray being played over a player with two arms just to draw people into the ball park. We felt it was unfair to do that when we were trying to win a pennant.[12]

Third baseman Mark Christman was more critical of Gray in his evaluation:

Pete Gray cost us the pennant in 1945. There were an awful lot of ground balls hit to him when he played center field. When the kids who hit those balls were pretty good runners, they could keep on going and wind up at second base. I know that lost us eight or ten ball games because it took away the double play or somebody would single and the runner on third would score, whereas if he had been on first it would take two hits to get him to score.[13]

Still other Brownie players were antagonistic towards Gray. On one occasion, Gray, who often asked a teammate to lend a hand when he was tying his shoes, called over pitcher Sig Jakucki. Never a big fan of Gray's and miffed over the recent release of his friend, Mike Kreevich, Jakucki stared at the rookie and snarled: "Tie your own goddamned shoes you one-armed son-of-a-bitch!"[14]

Like most players of the time, Gray was also a heavy drinker. Not surprisingly, the combined frustration of not being accepted by his teammates and questioning whether he was making the grade on his ability or his handicap, would often explode into a fistfight when Gray became inebriated.[15] On one occasion, after discovering that Jakucki had placed a dead fish in the pocket of his new sports coat, a drunken Gray floored the pitcher with a single punch.[16] Infielder Ellis Clary, who often tried to boost team morale with his self-deprecating sense of humor, admits that by August Gray's mere presence in the clubhouse created quite a bit of dissension simply because nobody knew how to treat him:

> I think Pete Gray was basically a good guy, but he had this terrible complex about his missing arm, and he resented it if he even thought you felt sorry for him. And he was always ready to fight. He didn't take guff from anybody. You'd feel sorry for the ornery son of a bitch if he didn't already make you hate his guts. None of that should take away from the fact that Pete could certainly play ball. He was no sideshow, but a damn good player. If he'd only had a better attitude, he might have been better accepted by the team."[17]

Although he was a flashy dresser off the field, Pete Gray was basically a shy person who felt uncomfortable with his instant celebrity status. Nor did he know how to handle it. If he happened to be seen with a Lucille Ball or a Bing Crosby off the field and then kept to himself in the clubhouse, his teammates considered him a show-off, too good to associate with them. If he turned in a good performance on the field and neglected to congratulate another teammate for a successful game, he was conceited, a selfish player who cared only about himself and not the team. If he rode the bench and brooded, he was a complainer, believing that "the world owed him a living." Simply put, it was a no-win situation for Pete Gray, regardless of how he handled himself. Therefore, he concentrated on the game—everything else was of secondary importance. According to Gray, there have been many exaggerated accounts of his personal disposition during his season with the Browns:

When I was with the Browns I sort of kept to myself. Vern Stephens and I were pretty close. We would go out for something to eat after the game. And Luke Sewell was good to me. But the other players had it that I was hard to get along wtih. Truth is, I came to the majors to play ball and to play to the best of my ability. That's what I was paid to do, that's what I worked my tail off for, and that's what I did. Nothing else really mattered, nor should it have mattered to anyone else.[18]

Manager Luke Sewell seemed to agree. Gray's scrappy, aggressive style of play and his competitive disposition endeared him to the Brownie skipper. If tension existed between the one-armed rookie and his team-mates, Sewell clearly overlooked it, claiming that he "never heard any resentment from the players about Gray or the publicity it received." Instead, years after their playing and managing days had ended, Sewell recalled Gray as "a friend to everybody":

If handling men was as easy as Pete, it would have been a breeze to manage. He was perfect, a real gentleman. He was cooperative and he went about his business. That is why Pete never worried the management like a lot of ball players do.

I will admit that I knew he couldn't last in the major leagues very long. Although he did a wonderful job—no, a remarkable job—with the facilities he had, the game is just too difficult for any one-armed man to play. I think, deep down, Pete realized he was being exploited. I surely thought so. That's why I didn't play him much. But as far as his personal behavior was concerned, I have nothing but good memories of him.[19]

On August 15 there was a shakeup in the front office. With the Browns firmly entrenched in seventh place and seemingly headed for another finish in the second division, Donald Barnes sold all his capital stock, which amounted to 31 percent of the club, to Richard Muckerman, a Brownie stockholder and owner of Polar Wave Ice and Fuel Company of St. Louis. Barnes had been president of the club since 1936 and had enjoyed his activities in the game, but by '45 he had become frustrated with the constant struggle of keeping the Browns out of bankruptcy. The sale of his holdings to Muckerman netted Barnes about $200,000, an offer he simply felt he could not refuse. In severing his connection with the Browns he claimed that he had accomplished "my three big ambitions: I finally saw a St. Louis American League pennant go up; I saw Sportsman's Park jammed on the last day of the '44 season; and I am leaving the Browns in sound financial condition."[20] Those close to the organization intimated however, that friction had developed between Barnes and the other stockholders over club policies and player person- nel, one of those players being Pete Gray.

With Muckerman as club president, the Browns' fortunes were on the rise while Gray's plummeted. The Brownie resurgence began with a mid–August homestand. They divided a six-game series with the Cleve- land Indians and followed it by taking three of four from the Athletics, three of five from the Senators, four straight from the Yankees, four of seven from the Red Sox, and five straight from the White Sox. During that homestand, the pitching staff of Hollingsworth, Jakucki, Muncrief, and Potter shone, reviving the Browns' chances for a pennant. Hol- lingsworth, in particular, turned in some sensational performances. He won six starts, two of them shutouts. The only loss he suffered in August was on the first day of the month against Detroit when his relief folded in the ninth. The 35-year-old veteran won a 3–0 shutout against Cleveland and followed it up with an 8–2 win over the Indians. Next he defeated the A's, 1–0, the Senators, 4–2, the Red Sox, 9–3, and the White Sox, 3–1.[21]

Behind the pitching of Hollingsworth, the impeccable defense of Gutteridge and Christman, and the heavy hitting of Stephens, McQuinn and Chet Laabs, the Browns played .773 ball in August. Their sensa- tional homestand lifted the club from a dismal seventh place standing, 10½ games out, to third place, only 4 games behind league-leading Detroit and 2 games behind second-place Washington. Gray, however, played sparingly.[22]

Unlike Barnes, Muckerman did not pressure Sewell into playing the one-armed rookie. In fact, the new owner's first action when he took con- trol of the club was to offer Sewell a new contract for '46 and underscore his full support for the Brownie manager. Sewell now had full authority to manage as he pleased. As a result, Gray played in only 10 games from mid–August to the end of the month, his most successful performance coming in an August 13 game against Washington in which he went two for three with a double that knocked in two runs to help his roommate Al Hollingsworth defeat the Senators, 4–2. His presence did not figure prominently in the outcome of another game until the opener of an August 30 doubleheader against Chicago when Gray collected four hits and knocked in the game-winning run. Between those two performances, the one-armed outfielder went hitless in all his other starts.[23] September was not much better. Gray was given an occasional starting role, but for

Gray slides home in the mud to score a run that put the Browns ahead of the Detroit Tigers in the eighth inning of a September 30th game. The Browns' momentary advantage was lost to a bases-loaded home run by Hank Greenberg just returned to baseball from military service. The game clinched the American League pennant for the Tigers. (Courtesy of Bettmann.)

most of the month he was a part-time player, coming off the bench to spot another outfielder or to do some pinch-hitting.[24]

Gray's major league baseball career was destined to end on V-J day when many of the game's stars returned from the battlefront. His last game on September 30, 1945, was the one that decided the pennant race between the Detroit Tigers and the Washington Senators. The Tigers, who were facing the third-place Browns in a doubleheader at Sportsman's Park, needed one game to win the American League race. The Senators, on the other hand, had completed their season a week earlier in second place. Two Tiger defeats would put them in the playoffs. Needless to say, the Washington fans were Brownie fans on that rainy September afternoon.

The Browns-Tigers game had already been postponed for three days because of inclement weather, and, though the rain continued to fall on September 30, transforming the ball field into a quagmire, the game had to be played. The World Series could no longer wait. Nelson Potter, the Browns' ace who had posted a 15–11 record during the '45 campaign, went to the mound against the Tigers' Virgil "Fire" Trucks, recently discharged from the Navy. What followed was one of the most exciting games of the World War II era.

In the bottom of the eighth inning with the score tied at two apiece, Gray reached first base on a fielder's choice. Hal Newhouser, the Tigers' ace, replaced Trucks to face Brownie first baseman George McQuinn. McQuinn doubled into right field and, as Tiger Roy Cullenbine played the ball, Gray took a risk and headed for home. Sliding headfirst across the plate, he barely beat the relay throw to score the go-ahead run in the game. Unfortunately, Gray's daring feat was not the game's deciding factor.

In the ninth inning Tigers' slugger Hank Greenberg, who had been discharged from the army earlier in the season, hit a grand slam to clinch the victory, 6–3, and the American League flag for Detroit. The Browns finished the season in third place, six games behind the Tigers.[25]

Pete Gray finished the season with a .218 batting average. In the 77 games in which he played, the one-armed outfielder collected 51 hits, 13 RBIs and scored 26 runs. What was most disappointing for the Browns, however, was that Gray stole only five bases for the entire season when they had counted on him for more.[26] Still, Gray, no matter what his team-mates claimed, could not be blamed for the Browns' failure to reclaim the pennant.

In 1944, when they captured their one and only flag, the Browns won just 89 games in a 154-game schedule. They managed to win with a .252 team batting average, second lowest in the American League. If not for the brilliant pitching they received from Galehouse and Potter down the stretch, the Browns would never have won the league championship.[27] It is no coincidence, however, that the Tigers who won the pennant in 1945 were a team very similar to the '44 Browns. Detroit won only 88 games, and its lineup did not have many feared hitters until Hank Greenberg returned from military service in September. Only one regular, Eddie Mayo, batted higher than .280. Hal Newhouser carried that team to the championship with a 25–9 record and a 1.81 ERA.[28] The wartime draft had thinned the American League of talent and created the opportunity for *both* of these clubs to capture the flag. If anything, the '45 Browns finish had little to do with Pete Gray, who did not enjoy regular playing time during the final two months of the season, and everything to do with the dismal way the club performed that year.

The '45 Browns were a mere shadow of their pennant-winning club of the previous year. The pitching staff slumped, with the exception of Bob Muncrief, who managed to collect another 13 victories. But the rest of the 1945 staff was mediocre at best: Jack Kramer, who went 17–13 in '44, fell to 10–15; Potter, who tallied a 19–7 record for the pennant winning club, fell to 15–11; Sig Jakucki went 13–9 in '44 but finished the '45 season at 12–10; and Tex Shirley, 5–4 for the pennant winners, fell to 8–12.

Even more so than in '44, the Brownie offense left much to be desired. With the exception of Vern Stephens, who led the AL with 24 homers and hit for a .289 average, no other regular hit above .277 or collected more than seven home runs. The team batting average dipped to .249, down three points from the previous season. The Browns also scored 87 fewer runs than they had in 1944.[30] Under these circumstances, it was more than a bit presumptuous to claim—as many Browns did—that Gray cost the club the AL pennant. The '45 Browns didn't deserve to win the league championship, and their mediocre statistics only reinforce that fact. Pete Gray had been made a scapegoat.

Playing Out the Dream

"You spend a good piece of your life gripping a baseball and in the end it turns out that it was the other way around all the time."—Jim Bouton, Ball Four, *(1970)*

GRAY MAY NOT have been included in the Browns' plans for 1946, but the club didn't let him slip away without getting its money's worth. Immediately after the '45 season ended, Charlie DeWitt, the publicity director for the Browns, took Gray on an eight-game barnstorming tour of the West Coast. The arrangements were explained to Gray as a goodwill gesture in reciprocation for his contributions to the Browns organization. In reality, DeWitt and his brother Bill, who served as the general manager of the club, had made a deal that would benefit both parties, though Gray's share was considerably more modest than the Browns.

For Gray, the profits from the barnstorming tour supplemented the meager salary he made with the Browns over the course of the season.

When Gray signed with the club in '44, his salary was about $4,000, the same pay that all rookies received. Recognizing the fact that Gray could be a box office attraction, however, the Browns inserted a bonus clause in the outfielder's contract whereby he would receive an additional $1,000 if the club did better at the gate than they did in their previous pennant-winning season. Although the Browns outpaced the Cardinals in attendance by nearly 160,000 fans through mid–July, they drew less and less as the season wore on, finishing the '45 campaign with a drop of approximately 25,000 attendance compared to '44. Under these circumstances, Gray wasn't entitled to the bonus, but Bill DeWitt gave it to him anyway. Even with the Browns' poor financial circumstances, $1,000 wasn't going to bankrupt the club and, indeed, Bill DeWitt was grateful to Gray for the box office draw he had produced. Besides, while Gray would earn an additional $5,400 for his part on the West Coast tour, the Browns would walk away with more than six times that amount in profits from that trip.[1] Had the one-armed rookie agreed to film the movie Charlie DeWitt had arranged for him to make in California, both parties would easily have doubled their earnings. But Gray refused.

Having heard that Monty Stratton of the Chicago White Sox had been paid $80,000 for his life's story, Gray's friends told him to hold out for more than the $15,000 he was being offered. While the money was attractive, Gray's integrity wouldn't allow him to do it. "They were going to pay me $15,000 for a few days' work on that film," recalled the balding rookie. "I've got to admit that the thing was appealing to me, too. But when the director told me that I'd have to wear a hair piece, I told him to forget the whole thing. No one was going to make a monkey out of me." Having rejected the movie proposal, Gray's total earnings from the Browns' organization amounted to just over $10,000.[2]

Shortly after their return from the West Coast trip, Bill DeWitt made arrangements to sell Pete Gray to the Toledo Mud Hens, the Browns' top farm club. The deal was completed on November 20, and Gray learned of his fate a day later over the radio. "I wasn't surprised that I was sent down," he admitted. "I figured I had a bad year, and I knew deep down I was going to be sent somewhere else. But I really didn't care. Even the salary didn't mean anything, as long as I was playing baseball and it was every day."[3] The truth is that he *did* care.

Throughout the winter, Ed Gilliland, president of the Mud Hens, tried to sign the one-armed outfielder to a contract. On one occasion he even traveled to Gray's hometown of Nanticoke to meet with him over the issue. Time and again Gray refused to settle for the $5,000 Gilliland was willing to pay. He repeatedly told the press, "If I don't play with Toledo, I don't know what I'll do. Maybe I'll go into some sort of business here in Nanticoke. But I'll forsake the game before giving in to those fellows this time around. I'm not going to sign a contract until I get what I think I'm worth."[4] When April rolled around and he still hadn't come to terms with Toledo, Gray began to reconsider his situation.

At 31 years of age, few if any clubs would be willing to take a chance on him, particularly now that the war was over and they could compete for the much younger talent that was flooding the minor leagues. Moreover, Gray realized that if he didn't sign within ten days after the opening of the regular season he would automatically become ineligible. With Gilliland standing firm on his offer, Gray decided to accept the $5,000 and ended his holdout on April 30, nine days into the regular season.[5] To be sure, the money itself was never the primary issue for Gray. Self-respect was. Gray wanted to play baseball on an everyday basis wherever he could, but he also wanted to make sure that he would never be taken advantage of again. He realized that professional baseball was a business and that salary was more than payment for services rendered; it was the only true measure of a player's worth. After the treatment he experienced in St. Louis, never really knowing where he stood, who could blame Pete Gray for placing a price on his value? Sadly, the contract dispute marked the beginning of the end for Pete Gray's professional baseball career.

In 1946 Gray appeared in only 48 games for the Mud Hens. Although he compiled a .925 fielding percentage in the outfield, he managed to hit just .250, 32 points higher than his previous season in the majors, but well below the .334 mark he had compiled in his three previous seasons in the minors. A year later, in 1947, Gray was suspended for failing to report to Toledo's spring training camp and decided to sit out the season.[6] When Gray requested reinstatement the following spring, Toledo assigned the one-armed outfielder to Class A Elmira of the Eastern League, a team that spent most of the '48 campaign in the cellar.[7] That season was a particularly difficult one for Gray, as he was the oldest player in a club that was in the process of rebuilding and he knew that he had a very limited future with it. Additionally, his comeback bid was hampered throughout the season by a strained hamstring that limited his playing time in the outfield. The 78 hits, 14 RBIs, and .290

average he compiled that season would have been a sign of great potential for most minor leaguers, but at the age of 33, it was a last blaze of glory for Pete Gray. He would end his professional baseball career the next season as a reserve outfielder for Dallas of the Texas league.

Nevertheless, those last three seasons were not without some memorable moments. On July 4, 1946, Gray went seven for seven, leading the Mud Hens to a doubleheader sweep of Columbus. In his Eastern League debut on May 17, 1948, the one-armed outfielder dazzled a crowd of 6,500 with his two hits and three RBIs in three at-bats.[8] Perhaps the most memorable were the pregame ceremonies held by the Wilkes-Barre Barons and Scranton Miners to honor Gray during Elmira's last regular season series with those clubs.[9]

On June 28, 1949, when he was given his outright release by Dallas, Pete Gray walked away from a very respectable, six-year minor league career. In the 472 games he played, the Gray collected 473 hits and 141 RBIs, with a .308 average. Although the 51 hits, 13 RBIs, and .218 average he compiled in his one season with the Browns was much less impressive, sportswriter Shirley Povich of the *Washington Post* put those statistics in proper perspective in a fitting epitaph to the one-armed outfielder's major league career: "What Gray might have accomplished in the big leagues if blessed with two arms is something for the imagination to play with. Surely he would have been one of the greatest big leaguers of all time."[10]

"Petey," Hometown
Folk Hero

"A guy who's played one game in the big leagues is like a former state senator. A big man in most neighborhoods and any saloon as long as he lives."– Wilfred Sheed, Diamonds Are Forever, *(1985)*

PENNSYLVANIA'S WYOMING VALLEY is a very different place today than it was at the turn of the nineteenth century when Eastern Europeans flooded its coalfields in search of the American Dream. Strip mining has destroyed the wild beauty of the land, unemployment continues to rise in a society that at one time could never find enough men to mine its coal, and there is widespread apathy among its youth over their prospects for the future. For small towns like Nanticoke, the death knell came in the 1960s when the Glen Alden Coal Company, realizing that it no longer controlled a viable industry, centralized its

125

operations elsewhere. Many who were still in the prime of their working years relocated in Philadelphia, New York, New Jersey, or New England, in search of gainful employment. Some returned to the Valley after their retirement, while others never did.

For all the change that came with the decline of a one-time booming anthracite industry, the Wyoming Valley remains essentially the same place. It is still a relatively safe haven from the vice, crime, and violence of the world beyond the Pocono Mountains. It is still the home of a passionate people who care about each other and their children. And it is still a place where natives return to find some peace of mind, an escape from the madness of the big city where they relocated years ago.

Not surprisingly, after his professional baseball career came to an end, Pete Gray returned to Hanover section of Nanticoke, just as he had done after the end of every season he spent in the pros. It was the only logical place to go. In Hanover he was—and still is—a "somebody." No matter how badly his career was failing after 1945, he was still the biggest celebrity in that part of town. When kids came running for his autograph, Pete would not only oblige them with his signature, he would take them to the local candy store and treat them. Even the adults seem to revere him for his determination to succeed in professional athletics, especially since he is "one of our own." No doubt about it, Pete Gray *owns* Hanover, because for one glorious summer a half century ago, he put that little hamlet on the map. And no one in town will ever forget that.

In Hanover (current population 3,044), Gray, who is now 80 years old, is still known as Petey, his childhood nickname. A lifelong bachelor, he still lives in the same white, double-block house his family built at the turn of the century. He still has the same friends he grew up with. Perhaps by choice, Pete Gray leads a very humble life—some would say a life of poverty. Since his one year in major league baseball did not qualify him for a pension, he managed to earn a modest income immediately after his retirement through a pool hall he owned and later by renting out the rooms of his own house. He admits that he struggled with a gambling addiction but was able to recover from it.[1] His days are spent walking the town and visiting with friends and neighbors. Most nights are spent at the local fire station shooting pool, playing cards, and watching whatever sporting contest happens to be in season. He used to play golf on a daily basis, usually shooting in the low 80s. However, major stomach surgery, the result of ulcers produced by years of heavy drinking, forced him to give up the game.[2] Stories about his golfing feats are legendary.

After his professional baseball career ended, Gray returned to his home town of Hanover, Nanticoke, Pennsylvania, where he inspired a young generation of baseball players. He is pictured here (kneeling in the dark warmup jacket) with a group of adolescent prospects. The gentleman kneeling to his left in the white shirt and tie is Pete Wyshner Sr., Gray's father. The Truesdale Breaker can be seen in the background. (Courtesy of John Barno.)

Thomas Heffernan, editor of the Wilkes-Barre *Sunday Independent*, still talks about the day thirty some years ago when he saw Pete's uncanny exhibition at a local driving range. "There he was, driving those balls far up on the hillside," recalled Heffernan. "But he wasn't teeing off on the ground like the rest of us. Instead he held a golf club—a wood—and a ball in his left hand, threw the ball in the air, and hit it far out not once but again and again." Similarly, Stephen Howryshko, a lifelong companion, tells of his first time out on a golf course with Gray: "'Hey, let's play for a buck a hole!' he said to me. I looked at him and replied, 'Well, Pete I really don't know. It's my first time out and I'm really not ready to play for money.' Three guys are ahead of us on the course and they evidently overheard our conversation, because I heard one of them say, 'Hey, the guy with one arm wants to play for money, Let's take him.' Pete walked away with thirty dollars that day, ten bucks from each one of those guys. He's just amazing, that one-armed son-of-a-gun!"[3]

The stories are tempered with some good-natured taunting, too. According to John Andrezejewski, another childhood friend and former golfing pal, "Pete's a regular gangster, the 'one-armed bandit' we call him. We make sure that his head doesn't swell too much by telling him that the year he played for the Browns there was nobody in baseball but black lung cases, 4-Fs, and some guy with one arm!"[4]

Gray enjoys the camaraderie as well as the bantering of his old friends. It was the only thing that got him through the hard times during his last few years in professional baseball and afterwards through a personal battle with alcohol. "I had trouble during those last few seasons in Toledo, Elmira, and Dallas," Gray admits. "Things weren't going so well on the playing field and the managers said I was difficult to handle because I held out for more money or I simply refused to report to spring training. Well, I guess I did. I didn't see any reason to report until a week before the season began, because I got myself mentally and physically prepared to play here in Hanover. It was nothing against the management, it was simply that I wanted to remain home among my friends for as long as I possibly could."[5]

For Gray, there had always been a sense of personal security among his friends, perhaps because they accepted him for the person he was and not a sideshow or a drawing card. When he confided in them, they listened. When he needed their help, they gave it without question. To this day, the dozen or so friends he has still protect him from the intrusive curiosity of outsiders. "My friends mean a lot to me," he confides. "I used to drink pretty heavy, lost weekends and that kind of thing. But they helped me get through it, and now I'm proud to say that I haven't taken a drink in twenty years. Maybe that's why I've always liked it here, being around my family and friends. Anyway, now that my playing days are over, there's no way I'm ever going to leave this place again!"[6]

Gray is the last remaining member of his immediate family. For years he played the roles of dutiful son and brother, taking care of his mother, who lived well into her nineties, and his older, semi-invalid brother Whitey, who passed away in the early 1980s. He does have nieces and nephews who live in Philadelphia and Connecticut, but the only relative who lives nearby is Bertha Vedor, a younger cousin who owns and operates a tavern in the town and serves as Pete's public relations person.

Bertha is a kind-hearted, comely woman who is extremely protective of Pete. Since he shuns publicity, refusing to have a phone installed in his own home, she takes all of his calls and will usually arrange whatever appointments he agrees to take with newspaper reporters, sportswriters or people from the entertainment business. She claims that "many

"Petey," as he is known to family and close friends is now a dapper 80 years of age. Although he was the subject of a 1986 television movie, "A Winner Never Quits," Gray shuns the limelight, preferring to lead a quiet existence among close friends and family. (Courtesy of the author.)

reporters who do come to interview Pete find him unsociable, defensive, and uncooperative" and explains that Pete's ambivalence towards publicity stems from his anger at being regarded as a "curiosity item" for such a long time, rather than the "extraordinary athlete he was."[7] That is why, over the years, he has turned down guest appearances on game shows such as *I've Got a Secret* and *What's My Line?* and more recently, on *Good Morning, America* and *Late Night with David Letterman.*[8] The list goes on. One gets the vivid impression that Gray is actually proud of all the limelight he rejects, opportunities other people would pay to have. There were three opportunities, however, that he did accept, albeit grudgingly. They were opportunities that proved to place his image in a better light with the general public.

The first was an interview with sportswriter Joe Falls of the *Detroit Free Press*. It resulted in one of the most entertaining and comprehensive stories ever written about Gray's career. When Falls initially contacted Gray over the phone in the winter of 1972, he became rather hostile:

> "I don't want to talk to anybody!" Gray snapped. "I just want to be left alone. I won't be here if you come," he added.
> Momentarily taken aback, Falls asked: "Where are you going to go?"
> "I'll go out and play golf," came the response.
> "Where are you going to play golf in mid-winter?" asked Falls.
> Gray retorted: "I'll find a place."
> But Falls refused to give in to the cantankerous disposition at the other end of the line and continued to spar with the former one-armed baseball player: "Well, I'll take my chances. I'll come anyway."
> "Don't bother because I'll go to Hershey."
> "Well then, I'll have to go to Hershey."
> "Then, I'll be in Allentown."
> "I'll take my chances." And with that, Joe Falls set out to find Pete Gray and talk with him about the Browns, the war years, and his current life.

When Falls arrived in Hanover, he found Gray to be a hesitant interviewee. But Bertha Vedor mediated the session at her house, giving her cousin the constant reassurance, "Now Petey, it's going to be all right." After explaining to Falls that Pete is a "little shy," she made a pot of coffee, set out a batch of brownies, and sat down to offer her support.

What transpired was an insightful article titled, "Once Upon a Time, There Was a One-Armed Outfielder. . . in the Major Leagues," which appeared in the January 1973 issue of *Sport Magazine*.[9] Falls later called the experience "one of the most memorable days of my life." Occasionally Gray would let down his guard and smile as he told the Detroit sportswriter some of the old stories about his days with the Browns. He even demonstrated how he could catch the ball and throw it. "I felt both

a sadness and an admiration for him," admitted Falls. "Sad that he was
such a forlorn and forgotten figure and pleased that I'd had the privilege
of seeing him in a major league uniform as a young boy warming up on
the sidelines in Yankee Stadium." Falls felt an unusual compassion for
Gray. Not so much because of his poverty or his unrefined manner, or
even because of his cantankerous, almost angry disposition, but because
baseball had treated him so poorly during his playing days and then
simply forgot about him.[10]

Falls made it his business to contact Kenneth Smith, one of the
curators at the National Baseball Hall of Fame, and convinced him to
acknowledge Gray's career by asking for one of the fielding mitts or
bats he used with the Browns. Perhaps these items could be put on
display as there might be some merit to showing the glove or bat used
by one of the very few men ever to play with one arm in the major
leagues.[11]

A year later, Smith made the phone call and asked for the glove, but
Pete refused to comply. It wasn't until 1989 that he finally sent the glove
to Cooperstown and it was promptly put on display, an enduring
testimony to his season in the majors.[12]

The second opportunity came in April 1978, when Avron B. Fogelman, the president of the Memphis Chicks baseball club and a prominent
civic leader, invited Gray to return to the Southern city where he made
his reputation. Having recently reestablished professional baseball in
Memphis after a nearly thirty year absence, Fogelman wanted the 1978
opening day ceremonies to be something special. "I wanted the first ball
to be thrown out by the most outstanding player that the Chicks ever
had," he claimed. "That player was Pete Gray."

For Fogelman, Gray represented "the most phenomenal accomplish-
ment that any baseball player has ever achieved." The fact that Gray was
so successful with just one arm was "incomprehensible for those who had
never seen him play."[13] After numerous phone conversations with the
former Chick, Fogelman finally persuaded him to accept the invitation.
On the evening of April 15, 1978, nearly 10,000 Memphians packed Tim
McCarver Stadium to honor their former star outfielder. Since the
ballpark had a seating capacity of only 5,500, the outfield had to be
roped off to accommodate all the fans.

In the pregame ceremony, Pete was lauded by the mayor of the city,
Fogelman, and the Memphis Chamber of Commerce, which presented
him with a plaque bearing the inscription:

Pete Gray
Most Valuable Player
Southern Association
1944

Hit .333 with 68 Stolen Bases
For the Memphis Chicks

Presented in Deep Appreciation
for his contribution to
Memphis Baseball

April 15, 1978

Before throwing out the ceremonial first pitch, Gray thanked the crowd with a short speech in which he recalled some of his teammates and the legendary manager Doc Prothro. He concluded: "It's good to be back in Memphis. I've got a lot of fond memories of this town since the fans were always great to me when I played here. Thank you for the two most wonderful years I enjoyed in professional basball."[14] The event had a profound impact on Gray. When he returned home to Hanover, Bertha recalled that he had tears in his eyes and all he could manage to say was, "I really didn't think they would remember me."[15]

The third opportunity will no doubt serve as the most enduring testimony to Pete Gray's example for generations to come. It occurred in 1986 when film producer James Keach approached Gray with the idea of making a television movie based on his life, titled, *A Winner Never Quits*. Gray had rejected similar offers on a number of previous occasions, but when Keach showed him the script and assured him that the movie would *not* focus on his handicap as much as it would on his determination as a baseball player who happened to have a handicap, Gray agreed. He was asked to advise actor Keith Carradine on any matters that might help in giving an accurate portrayal.[16] Their conversations took place over the phone since all of the outdoor filming was done in Chattanooga, Tennessee.[17] In fact it wasn't until the summer of 1993 that Gray finally met Carradine, who paid him a visit en route to an off-Broadway performance as Will Rogers in the Ziegfeld Follies.[18]

Carradine, who had starred in *Hair, Nashville, Choose Me*, and *Foxfire*, among other productions, proved to be a fine student. Not only did he pay close attention in his phone conversations with Gray, but he spent hours viewing an old 30 second film segment of the one-armed outfielder going through a pre-game warm up at Yankee Stadium. Carradine even enlisted the help of Nelson Gary Jr., the young boy who lost his arm and adopted Gray as his hero. "Nelson actually showed me Pete's manuever with his glove," admitted Carradine. "It was difficult to pick up because of the tendency to want to do it with my right hand. That problem was eliminated when I had my right arm strapped behind me for three hours at a clip. I had no choice then," he added.[19]

A *Winner Never Quits* first aired on ABC on the evening of April 14, 1986. It was a predictable but heart-warming story of a young boy's quest to fulfill his dream of playing in Yankee Stadium. At the beginning of the movie, a young Pete Wyshner despairs that his handicap will never allow him to realize his dream. Dennis Weaver, who plays the boy's immigrant father, does his best to raise his son's spirits, encouraging him to pursue that dream no matter how impossible it may appear. Pete's mother, played by Fionnula Flanagan, also stands by him, insisting that her older son Whitey (Andrew Lubeskie) look after him.

While Whitey trains to become a professional boxer, he encourages brother Pete to practice his footwork in order to achieve better balance and shows him how to hit and catch with the one arm. Slowly and painfully, the young boy begins to improve. The scene changes to adulthood and Pete has trouble breaking into minor league ball. When the Youngstown Bears need a left fielder, he hitchhikes to Ohio for a tryout, only to be told, "Sorry kid. Nothing personal. I couldn't hire you if you had asthma." Meantime, Whitey is pummeled so badly in a boxing match that he suffers permanent brain damage. The incident forces Pete to become more determined than ever to make it.

Carradine depicts Gray as a quiet, introverted type who doesn't reveal his true feelings to anyone. He dates a nurse who wants to get married and discourages Pete's dream of playing major league ball. But Gray has other plans. He ends any notion of marriage by telling her, "A weekend athlete doesn't make it to Yankee Stadium!"

Pete finally signs on with the Memphis Chicks. During the Memphis scenes Carradine skillfully displays Gray's talent for fielding and hitting. A romance also develops between the one-armed outfielder and a young waitress, Annie, played by Mare Winningham. But it is Gray's relationship with Nelson Gary Jr. (Huckleberry Fox) that steals the movie.

Producer James Keach was inspired by the relationship, having

Pete Gray shakes the hand of his youngest admirer—the author's son, Timothy. (Courtesy of the author.)

learned of it first-hand from his boyhood friend Nelson Gary, and pur-posely chose to build a subplot around it in the movie. The young boy's father (Charles Hallahan) who is concerned over his despondent child after he loses his arm, reads about Gray. In hopes of encouraging his son, he writes to the Chicks to arrange a meeting. Although Gray argues against it, the owner of the Memphis club sees the publicity value and orders the one-armed outfielder to cooperate. Eventually, Pete takes the boy under his wing and teaches him how to hit and throw and even a little bit about life itself. The climax of the film comes when Gray, now with the St. Louis Browns, finally makes it to Yankee Stadium, realizing his boyhood dream.

Of course, the telemovie was a fictionalized account based on Gray's life and as such had quite a few moments of sheer Hollywood dramatiza-tion. After viewing it, Gray, referring to the love interest played by Mare Winningham, remarked, "They really doctored it up, didn't they?" But then he later admitted, "Aw, I had my share of women in those days." The only difficulties Pete cited with the film was the fact that it never men-tioned his brother Tony and gave an inaccurate presentation of his response to Nelson Gary's visit. "I thought it should have mentioned my older brother Tony," said Gray. "He was the one who actually helped me with my baseball, not Whitey," he added. "As for the Gary boy, the movie suggested that I never wanted to meet him. That was totally false. I wanted to meet him. It was something special for me too. We developed a nice friendship and, in fact, I still stay in contact with him to this day." Overall, however, Gray was pleased with the movie and Carradine's gruff but mischievous portrayal of him.[20]

Today, baseball is still a big part of Pete Gray's life. Each year Yankee radio announcer Phil Rizzuto invites him to a game. Gray will usually attend and have lunch with the Hall of Famer but he insists on purchasing his own ticket. He is grateful to be remembered but refuses to be a burden to the former Yankee shortstop, despite Rizzuto's great admiration for him. But his greatest admirers are youngsters. "I get a lot of mail, mostly from kids requesting my autograph, and I answer every one of them, too," he says proudly.[21] Bertha Vedor agrees adding that, "Petey enjoys hearing from those kids since he meets the mailman promptly at 12 noon each day, the scheduled delivery time."[22] Gray really doesn't have to wait for the mail to know that he is remembered.

Whenever Gray attends the local Scranton Wilkes-Barre Red Barons games, he is surrounded by crowds of young girls and boys all wanting his autograph. He even comes prepared with a black felt tip pen and ends up signing dozens of baseballs. It doesn't end at the ballpark either. Fifty years after he completed his major league career, youngsters whose parents had not even been born when Gray played in the majors stop the one-armed man on the streets to ask for an autograph. They hear tales about his days in the big leagues or see *A Winner Never Quits* and ask, "How'd you ever play in the majors with one arm?" Peter just looks at them and says, "You know, son, there's a lot of guys with two good arms that don't make it!" After all is said and done, Pete Gray has the satisfaction of knowing that he is one of the very few who did.

Epilogue:
The Legacy of Pete Gray

FIFTY YEARS HAVE passed since Pete Gray platooned in the outfield of Sportsman's Park for the St. Louis Browns. In the interim the old concrete and steel-frame structure has given way to a more modern, multipurpose stadium. Nor do the Browns exist anymore. The 1953 season was their last in St. Louis. A year later they moved to Baltimore, where they changed their name to the Orioles and have since finished *first* in the American League on several occasions. So much more has changed about the game itself.

Today, baseball suffers an image problem. Its one-time heroes, the DiMaggios, Greenbergs, and Musials, have been replaced by anti-heroes, players more concerned about salary and ego than about becoming goodwill ambassadors for the game. They choose to define themselves by how much they make, not by *who* they are or how they perform on the field. That is why many of today's best players bicker about contracts, publish "kiss-and-tell" books, and even charge youngsters money for their autograph. The owners are no better. They wail about money from the day the World Series ends to the first day of spring training. Their motivation stems from the almighty dollar—how to create salary caps, limit free agency, and increase their own profit margins—rather than from a genuine feeling for the game. When both players and owners refuse to compromise, refuse to settle their financial differences out of a mutual respect for the integrity of the game, there is a lockout or a strike.

Sadly, these battles only serve to jeopardize the future of baseball among its most vital resource, the children. After all, baseball *is* a child's game, played for the enjoyment of the young imagination. It allows our children the opportunity to fulfill their fantasies, whether they be as grandiose as hitting a home run in the seventh and deciding game of the World Series, or the more modest dream of playing in Yankee stadium. But the game should also do for them what it did for their fathers and grandfathers, nurture a fundamental set of values such as self-discipline, perseverence, and commitment to a team effort. While only one in a million may get to wear a major league uniform, so many more can benefit from the intangible lessons of the game. Pete Gray always understood the importance of those lessons, for himself and for those youngsters he continues to inspire today.

Eight years after I began exploring his past, I finally understand why Pete opened himself to me in my childhood, why he asked me to "remember him when I made it to the big leagues." Like any youngster, I was too innocent to pass judgment on him. At age seven I had never read the baseball historians who wrote that Pete Gray was "no major leaguer, even by the slack standards of wartime," or that this one-armed hero of mine "knew he was in the majors primarily as a box office attraction." Instead, I granted him the one and only thing he ever wanted from anybody, the respect accorded to an athlete who had made it to the top in his chosen sport. More flattering was the fact that he honored me by requesting that I remember him when I made it to the big leagues. He respected *my* dream.

As an adult, I feel a special compassion for Pete Gray, especially now that I understand the personal pain and humiliation he must have felt when his St. Louis teammates quipped that he was nothing more than a curiosity item and one who had cost the Browns a chance to capture another pennant. Anyone who studied the statistics could see that it wasn't true, that the Browns had played better than .600 ball with Gray in their line-up and under .425 without him. Nevertheless, my hero carried that burden with him for many years after his playing days were over. If nothing else, I hope this book will ease that burden.

To be sure, Pete Gray owes no one any apology. After all, the sum of a man's life should *never* be judged by a set of statistics or what he might have failed to do, as much as by what he has done for others. By that measure, Pete Gray was—and still continues to be—a *hero* in every sense of the word. As a human being, he has demonstrated the ability to rise above the humble circumstances of his birth, and as a professional athlete, the determination to overcome the adversity of a physical disability. He always understood his limitations, but he never allowed them to get in the way of his success, nor prevent him from achieving beyond the realm of the ordinary.

No, Pete Gray was certainly not the first one-armed person to crack the majors—Hugh Daley, Cleveland's one-handed pitcher in the 1880s holds that distinction. Nor will he be the last to do so, since Jim Abbott of the New York Yankees has come to be respected for his pitching abilities. However, neither of these players had the opportunity to serve their country with the distinction that Gray displayed in 1945.

Pete Gray's respect for the game, his inspirational example on the playing field, and his humble efforts in the veterans' hospitals across the nation gave hope to dozens of American servicemen who returned home from the war as amputees. He also provided a role model for thousands of youngsters who aspired to big league stardom, whether they were physically disabled or not. In short Gray was a hero, for he embodied the ideals of hard work, perseverence, and faith in the American Dream. These are the very same values we always try to teach our children, but we never seem to find enough public personalities to reinforce our example. Perhaps that is why Hollywood was so eager to find Pete Gray in 1986 when it produced *A Winner Never Quits*. It proved to be a fitting testimony to the life of a man who never quit, no matter how many people quit on him. He beat the odds and won. Big time.

Fifty years after his major league career ended, Pete Gray continues to be a goodwill ambassador for the game. He reminds us of all that was good about baseball and its heroes and all that can be again, if we only pay attention to our hearts and to our dreams.

Pete Gray's Playing Statistics

(Real name: Peter J. Wyshner)

Born: March 6, 1915, Nanticoke, Pennsylvania

Batted left. Threw left. Height 6′ 1″. Weight 169.

Year	Club	League	Pos.	G	AB	R	H	2B	3B	HR	RBI	SB	Avg.
1942	Three Rivers	Can.-Am.	OF	42	160	31	61	5	0	0	13	5	.381
1943	Memphis	Southern	OF	126	453	56	131	7	6	0	42	13	.289
1944	Memphis	Southern	OF	129	501	119	167	21	9	5	60	68*	.333
1945	St. Louis	American	OF	77	234	26	51	6	2	0	13	5	.218
1946	Toledo	A.A.	OF	48	96	14	24	3	0	0	7	2	.250
1947	(Voluntarily Retired)												
1948	Elmira	Eastern	OF	82	269	37	78	7	2	0	14	5	.290
1949	Dallas	Texas	OF	45	56	18	12	2	0	0	5	5	.214
Major League Totals:				77	234	26	51	6	2	0	13	5	.218
Minor League Totals:				472	1535	275	473	45	17	5	141	98	.308

*League Leader

Endnotes

Introduction

1. Gray's critics include: Bill Gutman, *The Golden Age of Baseball, 1941–1963* (New York: Gallery Books, 1989), 30; Richard Goldstein, *Spartan Seasons: How Baseball Survived the Second World War* (New York: Macmillan, 1980), 209; David M. Jordan, *A Tiger in His Time: Hal Newhouser and the Burden of Wartime Ball* (South Bend, IN: Diamond Communications, Inc., 1990), 263; William B. Mead, *Baseball Goes to War* (Washington D.C.: Farragut Publishing Co., 1985), 209–11; Daniel Okrent and Harris Lewine,

The Ultimate Baseball Book (Boston: Houghton-Mifflin, Co., 1981), 221.

Pennsylvania's Wyoming Valley

1. For the early history of the Wyoming Valley, see Charles Miner, *History of Wyoming* (Philadelphia: n.p., 1845); Wesley Johnson, *Wyoming: A Record of the Commemorative Observance of the Battle and Massacre, 1778–1878* (Wilkes-Barre, PA: Wyoming Historical Society, 1882); Joseph J. Kelley, Jr., *Pennsylvania: The Col-*

onial Years, 1681–1776 (New York: Doubleday, 1980), 312–15; and Donald L. Miller & Richard E. Sharpless, *The Kingdom of Coal: Work, Enterprise, and Ethnic Communities in the Mine Fields* (Philadelphia: University of Pennsylvania Press, 1985), 6–10.

2. Oscar Handlin in his Pulitzer Prize winning work, *The Uprooted: The Epic Story of the Great Migrations That Made the American People* (New York: Grosset & Dunlap, 1951) was the first historian to concentrate of Eastern European assimilation into American life. He emphasized the importance of ethnic consciousness as an important first step in the assimilation process, particularly in urban areas where the members of the same ethnic group would congregate in order to translate their new American culture. A decade later, John Higham offered a more compelling argument by attributing nativism as the primary motivating force in forcing immigrants to assimilate. Nativist attitudes demanded that immigrants conform to traditional Protestant-American values See John Higham, *Strangers in the Land: Patterns of American Nativism, 1860–1925.* (New York: Atheneum, 1967) Michael Barendse, *Social Expectations & Perception: The Case of the Slavic Anthracite Workers* (State College, PA: Pennsylvania State University, 1981) and Victor Greene, *For God and Country: The Rise of Polish and Lithuanian Ethnic Consciousness in America, 1860–1910* (Madison, WI: Historical Society of Wisconsin,

1975) both agree with Higham's argument and apply it to the Polish and Lithuanian immigrants of northeastern Pennsylvania. They argue further that for these two ethnic groups, the assimilation process was interrupted by a split labor market divided along ethnic lines. This split labor market resulted in severe social animosities between these newly arrived Eastern Europeans and the members of the more established Northern European immigrants, most notably the English and Welsh.

3. Pete Gray, interview by author, September 20, 1988, Hanover section of Nanticoke, PA. See also William Wyshner (nephew of Pete Gray) interview by author January 15, 1993, New Canaan, CT.

4. Barendse, *Social Expectations*, 19–20, 25; and Miller & Sharless, *Kingdom of Coal*, 174–75.

5. Gray, interview, September 20, 1988; Wyshner, interview, January 15, 1993.

6. Miller & Sharpless, *Kingdom of Coal*, 3–5; and Barendse, *Social Expectations*, 22.

7. Commonwealth of Pennsylvania, *Report of the Department of Mines of Pennsylvania*, Part I– Anthracite (Harrisburg, PA: Commonwealth of Pennsylvania, 1924), 18 (hereafter referred to as "Mine Reports"). The most accurate records of total production, numbers of workforce, and fatalities for Pennsylvania's anthracite coal fields were provided in these reports beginning in 1870.

8. Victor Greene, *The Slavic*

Community on Strike: Immigrant Labor in Pennsylvania Anthracite (South Bend, IN: Notre Dame University, 1968), 2–3. See also Barendse, *Social Expectations*, 226; and Robert J. Casey & W.S. Douglas, *The Lakawanna Story* (New York: n.p., 1951), 145–49.

9. Greene, *Slavic Community*, 3.

10. Robert Janosov (professor of history, Community College of Luzerne County), interview by author, November 19, 1991, Nanticoke, PA. See also Janosov, "The Auchincloss Mine Disaster of 1904" (Unpublished paper, Community College of Luzerne County, 1989).

11. *Mine Reports* (1923), 12–13; and Janosov, "Auchincloss Disaster," 4.

12. Janosov, interview, November 19, 1991.

13. Pete Gray, interview by author, May 2, 1989; and Edward Sincavage (neighbor, childhood friend and teammate of Gray), interview by author, May 1, 1991, Alden, PA.

14. Gray, interview, May 2, 1989; see also Ed Perluke (childhood friend of Gray), interview by author, October 20, 1989, Hanover section of Nanticoke, PA; and John Barno (childhood friend, neighbor and teammate of Gray), interview by author, May 1, 1991, Hanover section of Nanticoke, PA.

15. Miller & Sharpless, *Kingdom of Coal*, 186–87.

16. William C. Kashatus, M.D. (childhood resident of Hanover), interview by author, November 18,

1991, Lake Silkworth, PA; Michael & Stephen Howryshko (childhood friends of Gray), interview by author, November 19, 1991, Hanover section of Nanticoke, PA.

17. Gray, interview, May 2, 1989; Howryshko, interview, November 19, 1991; Sincavage, interview, May 1, 1991; Perluke, interview October 20, 1989; and Tony Burgas (childhood friend and teammate of Gray), interview by author May 30, 1991, Hanover section of Nanticoke, PA.

18. Joseph Lawler, "Northeastern Pennsylvania Has Been a Baseball Hotbed," *Phillies Report* (February 19, 1987. 16–17; and Lawler, "Coal Town Baseball: The Major Leagues and Northeastern Pennsylvania," *Pennsylvania Magazine* (Summer 1986): 27–30.

19. Mike Shatzkin, *The Ballplayers* (New York: William Morrow, 1990), 228–29, 524–25.

20. Lawler, "Northeast Pennsylvania Hotbed," 17.

21. Joseph Lawler, "Freeman's Power Hitting Bucked Turn-of-the-Century Trend," *Red Sox Fan News* (May 27, 1986): 18, 22.

22. Janosov, interview, November 19, 1991.

23. Janosov, "Model Company Housing for Anthracite Workers in an Age of Industrial Efficiency: The Case of Concrete City," *Canal History & Technological Proceedings* edited by Lance E. Metz (Harrisburg, PA: Center for Canal History, 1986): 223–41.

24. Miller & Sharpless, *Kingdom of Coal*, 121–25.

25. *Mine Reports* (1905), xi; see

also Janosov, "Auchincloss Mine Disaster," 2.

26. Barendse, *Social Expectations*, 15–17.

27. Ibid., 53–56.

28. *Mine Reports* (1901), 12; see also Barendse, *Social Expectations*, 23, 25.

29. *Wilkes-Barre Record*, November 18, 1933, 14.

Losing an Arm, Committing to a Dream

1. Gray, interview by author, June 26, 1989; Bertha Vedor (cousin and personal secretary of Gray) interview by author, May 2, 1991, Hanover section of Nanticoke, PA; Perluke, interview, October 20, 1989.

2. Gray, interview, June 26, 1989; Wyshner interview: January 15, 1993.

3. Gray, interview, June 26, 1989; Howryshko, interview, November 19, 1991.

4. Gray, interview, June 26, 1989.

5. Barno, interview, May 1, 1991.

6. Gray quoted in the following accounts: *USA Today*, April 28, 1989, 1C–2C; William Mead, *Baseball Goes to War* (Washington D.C.: Farragut Publishing Co., 1985), 207; *Dallas Morning News*, April 10, 1983, 16-B; Richard Goldstein, *Spartan Seasons: How Baseball Survived the Second World War* (New York: Macmillan, 1980), 208; and Joe Falls, "Once Upon a Time There Was a One-Armed

Outfielder. . . in the Major Leagues," *Sport Magazine* (January 1973): 23–24.

7. Gray, quoted in *Dallas Morning News*, April 10, 1983, 16-B; and *New York Daily News*, August 7, 1971, 21.

8. Gray, quoted in Falls, "Once Upon a Time," 86.

9. Perluke, interview, October 20, 1989; see also *The Sporting News*, March 22, 1945, 6.

10. Gray, interview by author August 8, 1989; also Gray quoted in *Dallas Morning News*, April 10, 1983; and *New York Daily News*, August 7, 1971, 21.

11. Gray, interview, August 8, 1989; Howryshko, interview, November 19, 1991.

12. Statistics and record-breaking events regarding baseball in the 1920s taken from David Nemec et. al. *Twentieth Century Baseball Chronicle: A Year-by-Year History of Major League Baseball* (New York: Beekman House, 1991); and Rick Wolff, editor, *The Baseball Encyclopedia* (8th edition, New York: Macmillan, 1990).

13. Gray, interview, August 8, 1989; also Gray quoted in *The Sporting News*, March 22, 1945, 6.

14. Gray, interview, August 8, 1989; also Gray quoted in *Toronto Star Weekly*, April 13, 1983, 22.

15. George Staller quoted in Harrington E. Crissey, Jr., *Teenagers, Graybeards and 4-F's: The American League* (Trenton, NJ: White Eagle Printing Co., 1982), 120.

16. Al Cihocki quoted in Crissey, *Teenagers, Graybeards and 4-Fs*, 58.

17. Gray, interview, August 8,

1989; Also see Gray quoted in Crissey, *Teenagers, Graybeards and 4-Fs*, 135.

18. Sincavage, interview, May 1, 1991; Barno interview, May 1, 1991; Burgas interview, May 30, 1991.

19. *Wilkes-Barre Times Leader*, July 10, 1933, 20.

20. Barno, interview, May 1, 1991.

21. Gray, interview by author, October 20, 1989; Howryshko, interview, November 19, 1991; Kashatus, interview, November 18, 1991.

22. Bill Rabinowitz, "Baseball and the Great Depression," *Baseball History* edited by Peter Levine (Westport, CT: Meckler Books, 1989), 54–55.

23. Burleigh Grimes, quoted in *The Sporting News*, February 5, 1931, 8.

24. Rabinowitz, "Baseball and Depression," 51.

25. *Wilkes-Barre Times Leader*, May 7, 1934, 6; May 14, 1934, 6; June 4, 1934; 16; and August 20, 1934, 14.

26. Gray, interview, October 20, 1989.

27. Burgas, interview, May 30, 1991.

28. *Wilkes-Barre Times Leader*, May 2, 1935, 21; May 3, 1935, 24; May 10, 1935, 30.

29. *Wilkes-Barre Times Leader*, May 7, 1935, 10; May 9, 1935, 1; June 3, 1935, 10; and June 7, 1935, 1, 22.

30. Vincent Znaniecki, quoted in John Bodnar, *Anthracite People. Families, Unions & Work, 1900–1940*

(Harrisburg, PA: Pennsylvania Historical and Museum Commission, 1983), 96–98.

31. Gray, interview by author, February 6, 1990; Howryshko, interview, August 9, 1991.

32. *Wilkes-Barre Times Leader*, May 4, 1936, 18.

33. *Wilkes-Barre Times Leader*, May 11, 1936, 16.

34. *Wilkes-Barre Times Leader*, June 29, 1936, 17.

35. *Wilkes-Barre Times Leader*, August 3, 1936, 18.

36. *Wilkes-Barre Times Leader*, September 7, 1936, 15.

37. *Wilkes-Barre Times Leader*, September 14, 1936, 16.

38. *Wilkes-Barre Times Leader*, September 21, 1936, 17.

39. *Wilkes-Barre Times Leader*, September 28, 1936, 18.

40. *Wilkes-Barre Times Leader*, July 8, 1937, 17.

41. *Wilkes-Barre Times Leader*, August 21, 1937, 20.

Road to the Pros

1. Barno, interview, May 1, 1991.

2. Burgas, interview, May 30, 1991.

3. Gray, interview by author, March 8, 1990; see also Gray quoted in Crissey, *Teenagers, Graybeards, & 4-Fs*, 135; and *St. Paul Sunday Pioneer Press*, March 21, 1982, 4.

4. Gray, interview, March 8, 1990; see also Gray quoted in *USA Today*, April 28, 1989, 2C.

5. Gray, interview, March 8, 1990; see also Gray quoted in Mead, *Baseball Goes to War*, 207–8; and

Toronto Star Weekly, March 24, 1945, 11.

6. Gray, interview, April 20, 1990; see also Gray quoted in David Pietrusza, *Baseball's Canadian-American League* (Jefferson, NC: McFarland & Company, Inc., 1990), 156.

7. Pietrusza, *Can-Am League*, 18–19, 42–50, 52–57, 85.

8. Ed Yasinski, quoted in Pietrusza, *Can-Am League*, 48.

9. Bill Fennhahn, quoted in Pietrusza, *Can-Am League*, 47.

10. Gray, interview, April 20, 1990.

11. Barney Hearn, quoted in Pietrusza, *Can-Am League*, 156.

12. Ibid.

13. Ibid.

14. *Wilkes-Barre Times Leader*, August 19, 1938, 17.

15. Pietrusza, *Can-Am League*, 160–62.

16. *Toronto Star Weekly*, April 12, 1943, 12.

17. Mead, *Baseball Goes to War*, 208.

Baseball Goes to War

1. Bill Gilbert, *They Also Served: Baseball and the Homefront, 1941–1945* (New York: Crown Publishers, 1992); Goldstein, *Spartan Seasons*; and Mead, *Baseball Goes to War* are the finest accounts on baseball during the World War II era and provided valuable references for this book.

2. Judge Kenesaw Mountain Landis, quoted in Gilbert, *They Also Served*, 41; see also Bill

Gutman, *The Golden Age of Baseball, 1941–1963* (New York: Gallery Books, 1989), 22.

3. Franklin D. Roosevelt, quoted in Gilbert, *They Also Served*, 42.

4. Mead, *Baseball Goes to War*, 87–88.

5. Gutman, *Golden Age*, 22.

6. Mead, *Baseball Goes to War*, 49.

7. Mead, *Baseball Goes to War*, 96–97.

8. Hank Greenberg, *The Story of My Life*, edited by Ira Berkow (New York: Times Books, 1989), 145.

9. Ibid., 148–49; and Mead, *Baseball Goes to War*, 33.

10. Gray, interview by author, June 13, 1990.

11. Bert Shepherd, quoted in *Philadelphia Inquirer*, September 18, 1992, C-1, C-6.

12. Joe Nuxhall, quoted in Gilbert, *They Also Served*, 143–44.

13. Gray, interview, June 13, 1990.

14. Harrington Crissey, quoted in John Thorn and Pete Palmer, editors, *Total Baseball* (New York: Warner Books, Inc., 1989), 24.

15. Goldstein, *Spartan Seasons*, xiii.

16. Mead, *Baseball Goes to War*, 195–98.

17. Ibid., 3.

18. Ibid., 3–4.

19. Ibid.

20. Ibid.

21. Ibid., 79–80.

22. Ibid., 73.

23. Goldstein, *Spartan Seasons*, 97.

24. Mead, *Baseball Goes to War*, 78–79.

25. Gene Schoor, *The History of the World Series* (New York: William Morrow, 1990), 191–94.

26. William Manchester's *The Glory and the Dream* (New York: Banam Books, 1975), 289–328, provides a fine social history of the American homefront during the World War II era.

27. Gilbert, *They Also Served*, 6–7.

MVP of the Southern Association

1. Mickey O'Neill, quoted in *Toronto Star Weekly*, March 24, 1945, 11.

2. *St. Louis Post-Dispatch*, December 12, 1944, 12; and *Memphis Press-Scimitar*, September 29, 1944, 17.

3. See Memphis Chicks Baseball Club, "Tradition: Chicks' Hallmark," *Memphis Chicks 1978 Yearbook* (Memphis, TN: Memphis Chicks Baseball Club, 1978), 32–33, 35.

4. Gray, interview by author, March 6, 1991.

5. Doc Prothro, quoted in *Wilkes-Barre Times Leader*, May 24, 1943, 11; see also *Memphis Commercial Appeal*, April 16, 1978, 12.

6. Prothro quoted in *Detroit Free Press*, March 14, 1945, 14.

7. Ibid., see also Prothro quoted in *Toronto Star Weekly*, May 12, 1945, 12.

8. *St. Louis Post-Dispatch*, August 20, 1944, 7.

9. Gray, quoted in *Toronto Star Weekly*, March 24, 1945, 11; see also *The Sporting News*, February 8, 1945, 13.

10. Pete Gray, interview by author, July 29, 1990; see also *New York American*, September 17, 1944, 15; *Wilkes-Barre Times Leader*, September 19, 1944, 13; *Wilkes-Barre Times Leader*, December 18, 1944, 12.

11. Gray, interview, July 29, 1990.

12. Ibid.

13. Howryshko, interview, November 19, 1991.

14. *Time Magazine*, June 12, 1944, 78.

15. *The Sporting News*, August 17, 1944, 25; August 31, 1944, 26; September 14, 1944, 24.

16. Gray quoted in *Memphis Commercial Appeal*, April 16, 1978, 12.

17. *The Sporting News*, August 17, 1944, 25; October 12, 1944, 10.

18. Wish Egan, quoted in *Toronto Star Weekly*, May 12, 1945, 12.

19. *The Sporting News*, September 14, 1944, 24.

20. *Toronto Star Weekly*, March 24, 1945, 11.

21. Goldstein, *Spartan Seasons*, 209; Bill Borst, *Last in the American League* (St. Louis: Krank Press, 1978), 84; and *Washington Post*, May 31, 1945, 8.

22. Gray's statistical totals can be found on page 198. These were compiled by the research staff at the National Baseball Hall of Fame and Museum.

23. Gray, quoted in *The New*

York Times, September 30, 1944,
24; *The Sporting News*, September
21, 1944, 9; and *St. Louis Post-
Dispatch*, January 4, 1945, 16.

24. Edward Barry, quoted in
Wilkes-Barre Times Leader,
December 18, 1944, 12.

25. Ibid.

Last in the American League . . . Until 1944

1. Bill Borst, *Baseball Through
a Knothole: A St. Louis History* (St.
Louis: Krank Press, 1980), 94–95.
The most definitive account on the
'44 season is Borst's recently
published book, *The Best of
Seasons: The 1944 St. Louis Cardinals and St. Louis Browns* (Jefferson, NC: McFarland & Company,
Inc., 1995).

2. For the most complete ac-
count on the Browns' history see
Bill Borst, *Still Last in the
American League; The St. Louis
Browns Revisited*. (West Bloomfield,
MI: Altwerger & Mandel Publishing
Co., 1992).

3. Bobo Newsom, quoted in
William J. Miller, "Still Pulling for
the Browns," *The Brown Stocking*,
edited by Bill Borst (2 vols., St.
Louis: Browns Fan Club, 1985), I,
15.

4. Borst, *Still Last in A.L.*, 17.

5. Luke Sewell, quoted in
Crissey, *Teenagers, Graybeards &
4-Fs*, 134.

6. Borst, *Still Last in A.L.*,
66–76; Mead, *Baseball Goes to
War*, 129–88.

7. Ibid.

8. George McQuinn, quoted in
Mead, *Baseball Goes to War*, 136.

9. Don Gutteridge, interview by
author, October 25, 1989, Pittsburgh, KS.

10. Luke Sewell, quoted in
Mead, *Baseball Goes to War*, 136.

11. Eugene Murdock, "Joe and
Luke: The Sewell Story," *Baseball
History*, edited by Peter Levine
(Westport, CT: Meckler Books,
1989), 37–47.

12. Luke Sewell, quoted in *The
Sporting News*, October 5, 1944,
14.

13. Mead, *Baseball Goes to War*,
165–72.

14. Ibid., 173–76; Borst, *Still
Last in A.L.*, 70–71.

15. Mead, *Baseball Goes to War*,
179.

16. Ibid., 180; Borst, *Still Last
in A.L.*, 73.

17. Mead, *Baseball Goes to War*,
180.

18. Ibid., 182–86; Borst, *Still
Last in A.L.*, 74–75.

19. Nelson Potter, interview by
author, August 15, 1989, Mount
Morris, Il.

20. Marty Marion, quoted in
Mead, *Baseball Goes to War*, 187.

Living the Dream as a St. Louis Brown

1. Donald Barnes, quoted in
Washington Post, May 31, 1945, 8.

2. Charles DeWitt, quoted in
The Sporting News, November 23,
1944, 1–2.

3. Luke Sewell, quoted in *The
Sporting News*, March 22, 1945, 6.

4. Ibid.

5. Ibid.

6. Gray, quoted in *The Sporting News*, March 22, 1945, 6.

7. Ibid.

8. Ibid.

9. *The Sporting News*, April 12, 1945, 3.

10. Sewell quoted in *The Sporting News*, March 15, 1945, 4.

11. Potter, interview, August 15, 1989.

12. *The Sporting News*, April 26, 1945.

13. Box scores for all six games of the 1945 Browns-Cardinals preseason series were published in *The Sporting News*, April 12, 1945, 22; April 19, 1945, 4, 19; and April 26, 1945, 14.

14. *St. Louis Post-Dispatch*, April 20, 1945, 12.

15. Al Hollingsworth, interview by author, November 5, 1989, Austin, TX.

16. Gutteridge, interview, October 25, 1989.

17. Gray, interview, March 6, 1991; and Falls, "Once Upon a Time," 86.

18. *The Sporting News*, May 3, 1945, 14, 16.

19. *The Sporting News*, May 10, 1945, 15; May 17, 1945, 13.

20. Hollingsworth, interview, November 5, 1989.

21. Gutteridge, interview, October 25, 1989.

22. Gray, interview, March 6, 1991.

23. Luke Sewell, quoted in *Washington Post*, May 31, 1945, 8.

24. *The Sporting News*, June 7, 1945, 16.

25. Gray, quoted in Falls, "Once Upon a Time," 86.

26. Gray, interview, March 6, 1991; see also Gray quoted in *The Sporting News*, June 28, 1945, 5.

27. Gray, quoted in *The New York Times*, May 27, 1945, 22.

28. Falls, "Once Upon a Time, 87; see also *USA Today*, April 28, 1989, 2C.

29. *The Sporting News*, June 31, 1945, 17.

30. *Cleveland Plain Dealer*, June 12, 1945, 18.

31. *The Sporting News*, March 22, 1945, 6.

32. Mead, *Baseball Goes to War*, 209; see also *Dallas Morning News*, April 10, 1983, 16B.

33. *The Sporting News*, June 28, 1945, 5; and *Washington Evening Star*, November 24, 1945, 12.

34. *Washington Post*, May 31, 1945, 8.

35. *The Sporting News*, May 3, 1945, 16.

36. *The Sporting News*, June 7, 1945, 9.

Reversal of Fortune

1. *The Sporting News*, June 28, 1945, 5.

2. *USA Today*, April 28, 1989, 1C.

3. Ed Lopat, quoted in Crissey, *Teenagers, Graybeards and 4'Fs*, 53.

4. Jimmy Dykes, quoted in Crissey, *Teenagers, Graybeards and 4-Fs*, 43.

5. Goldstein, *Spartan Seasons*, 209.

6. *The Sporting News*, July 12, 1945, 17.

7. Ibid.

8. *St. Louis Post-Dispatch*, July 5, 1945, 12.

9. *St. Louis Post-Dispatch*, July 8, 1945, 14.

10. Ibid.

11. Mike Kreevich, quoted in Mead, *Baseball Goes to War*, 210.

12. George McQuinn, quoted in Crissey, *Teenagers, Graybeards and 4-Fs*, 143.

13. Mark Christman, quoted in Mead, *Baseball Goes to War*, 209–10.

14. Sig Jakucki, quoted in *Baseball's Greatest Quotations*, edited by Paul Dickson (New York: Harper Collins, 1991), 205.

15. *Dallas Morning News*, April 10, 1983, 16B.

16. *Chicago Tribune*, April 20, 1989, 3; and *Wilkes-Barre Times Leader*, April 15, 1967, 10.

17. Ellis Clary, quoted in *Dallas Morning News*, April 10, 1983, 16B.

18. Pete Gray, interview by author, July 18, 1991.

19. Sewell, quoted in Crissey, *Teenagers, Graybeards and 4-Fs*, 134.

20. *The Sporting News*, August 16, 1945, 5.

21. *The Sporting News*, August 30, 1945, 9.

22. Ibid.

23. *The Sporting News*, August 23, 1945, 14; August 30, 1945, 17–18; and September 6, 1945, 15.

24. *The Sporting News*, September 13, 1945, 15–16; September 20, 1945, 13; September 27, 1945, 15.

25. *The Sporting News*, October 4, 1945, 27; see also *Gutman, Golden Age*, 31–32.

26. Mead, *Baseball Goes to War*, 209.

27. For statistical data on the 1944 and 1945 St. Louis Browns and Detroit Tigers, see David S. Neft, et al., *The Sports Encyclopedia: Baseball* (New York: Grosset & Dunlap, 1976), 230.

28. Ibid., 234.

29. Ibid.

30. Ibid.

Playing Out the Dream

1. *St. Louis Post-Dispatch*, November 20, 1945, 15.

2. Mead, *Baseball Goes to War*, 210.

3. Gray, interview, July 18, 1991.

4. Gray, quoted in the following: *St. Louis Post-Dispatch*, September 21, 1945, 14; *Wilkes-Barre Times Leader*, November 20, 1945, 12; *The New York Times*, November 21, 1945, 21; *Wilkes-Barre Times Leader*, February 6, 1946, 14.

5. *Wilkes-Barre Times Leader*, April 30, 1946, 13.

6. Mead, *Baseball Goes to War*, 211.

7. *Wilkes-Barre Times Leader*, May 18, 1948, 14.

8. *St. Louis Post-Dispatch*, May 18, 1948, 21.

9. *Wilkes-Barre Record*, September 1, 1948, 19.

10. *Washington Post*, July 9, 1945, 8.

"Petey," Hometown Folk Hero

1. Gray, quoted in *New York Daily News*, August 7, 1971, 21.

2. *USA Today*, April 28, 1989, 1C.

3. Thomas Heffernan, quoted in *Wilkes-Barre Sunday Independent*, July 30, 1989, Sec. 3, 12.

4. John Andrezewski, quoted in *USA Today*, April 28, 1989, 2C.

5. Gray, interview by author, August 13, 1992.

6. Ibid., see also *St. Paul Sunday Pioneer Press*, March 21, 1982, 1C; Falls, "Once Upon a Time," 87.

7. Bertha Vedor, interview by author, May 2, 1991.

8. *Wilkes-Barre Times Leader*, July 3, 1985, 1C, 5C.

9. Falls, "Once Upon a Time."

10. *The Sporting News*, May 19, 1973, 2, 4.

11. Ibid.

12. *USA Today*, April 28, 1989, 2C.

13. Avron B. Fogelman, interview by author, June 14, 1993, Memphis, TN.

14. Gray, quoted in *Memphis Commercial Appeal*, April 16, 1978, 12.

15. Vedor, interview, May 2, 1991.

16. *Wilkes-Barre Times Leader*, April 16, 1986, 1C, 12C.

17. *New York Daily News*, March 31, 1986, 23.

18. Gray, interview, August 13, 1992.

19. Keith Carradine, quoted in *New York Daily News*, April 14, 1986, 20; and *New York Post*, April 14, 1986, 17.

20. Gray, interview by author, June 10, 1993; see also Gray quoted in *Wilkes-Barre Times Leader*, April 16, 1986, 12C.

21. Gray, interview, June 10, 1993.

22. Vedor, interview, May 2, 1991.

Bibliography

During the fifty years since Pete Gray played for the St. Louis Browns there has been just one book written about him. It was a children's book titled *Pete Gray, One-Armed Major Leaguer* written by William G. Nicholson and illustrated by Ray Abel (Prentice-Hall, 1976). Nicholson had completed a much more extensive manuscript on Gray's life but only managed to have one brief interview with the former Brown, something which discouraged him from publishing a longer treatment. I was more fortunate.

Over the six year period from 1988 to 1993, I was able to earn Pete Gray's trust and friendship. In return, he told me much about his life. He became the primary source of information for this book.

Contemporary periodicals were also very useful. The best of these sources is *The Sporting News*, which during the 1940s provided a full column on each major league team every week of the season. It also included summaries of minor league action and notable minor league performances, the boxscore of every major league game, and feature articles on both major and minor league players and games of special interest. It was indispensable for my research on Gray's minor league seasons with the Memphis Chicks, as well as the '45 season with the St. Louis Browns.

153

Other periodicals included *Baseball Digest, The Chicago Tribune, The Christian Science Monitor, Dallas Morning News, Memphis Commercial Appeal, Memphis Press Scimitar, The New York Times, Sports Illustrated, St. Louis Post-Dispatch, Toronto Star Weekly, Washington Evening Star, The Washington Post, Wilkes-Barre (Pennsylvania) Record, Wilkes-Barre (Pennsylvania) Sunday Independent*, and the *Wilkes-Barre (Pennsylvania) Times Leader*. In addition, I found *The Baseball Encyclopedia*, published by Macmillan (eighth edition, 1990), and *The Ballplayers*, edited by Mike Shatzkin (New York: William Morrow, 1990), to be invaluable reference works for major and minor league statistics as well as biographical vignettes of former professional ballplayers. Other selected books and articles which were especially valuable included the following:

Bodnar, John. *Anthracite People: Families, Unions & Work, 1900–1940*. Harrisburg, PA: Pennsylvania Historical Commission, 1983.

Borst, Bill. *Baseball Through A Knothole: A St. Louis History*. St. Louis: Krank Press, 1980.

_____. *Still Last in the American League: The St. Louis Browns Revisited*. West Bloomfield, MI: Altwerger & Mandel, 1992.

Cavanaugh, Jack. "Recalling Heyday of Pete Gray, One-Armed Baseball Star of the '40's." *Dallas Morning News*, Sunday, April 10, 1983, p. 16B.

Cooper, Joe. "Recalling Pete Gray in His Gloried Semi-pro Days." *Wilkes-Barre Sunday Independent*, July 30, 1989, Section 3, p. 12.

Crissey, Harrington E., Jr. *Teenagers, Graybeards, and 4-Fs. Volume II: American League*. Trenton, NJ: White Eagle, 1982.

Dexter, Charles. "Baseball's One-Armed Wonder." *Toronto Star Weekly*, March 24, 1945, p. 11.

Falls, Joe. "Once Upon a Time There Was a One-Armed Outfielder . . . in the Major Leagues." *Sport Magazine*, (January 1973): 23–6, 86–7.

Falls, Joe. "A Visit with Pete Gray." *The Sporting News*, May 19, 1973, pp. 2, 4.

Fox, John W. "Pete Gray Remembers." *USA Today*, Friday, April 28, 1989, Section C, pp. 1–2.

Gilbert, Bill. *They Also Served: Baseball and the Homefront, 1941–1945*. New York: Crown, 1992.

Goldstein, Richard. *Spartan Seasons: How Baseball Survived the Second World War*. New York: Macmillan, 1980.

Greene, Victor R. *For God and Country. The Rise of Polish and Lithuanian Consciousness in America, 1860–1910*. Madison, WI: State Historical Society of Wisconsin, 1975.

_____. *The Slavic Community on Strike: Immigrant Labor in Pennsylvania Anthracite*. South Bend, IN: University of Notre Dame, 1968.

Hendrickson, Robert. "How Pete Gray Defied the Odds." *Baseball Digest*, (April 1971): 74–79.

Holtzman, Jerome. "One-Armed Pete Gray's Career Was Short and Bitter." *Chicago Tribune*, Thursday, April 20, 1989, Section 4, p. 3.

Kashatus, Bill. "A Season in the Sun. World War II Baseball, the 1945 St. Louis Browns, and a One-Armed Outfielder Named Gray." *Gateway Heritage*, (Summer 1991): 38–49.

Lawler, Joseph. "Coal Town Baseball. The Major Leagues and Northeastern Pennsylvania." *Pennsylvania Magazine* 5, no. 2 (1988): 27–30.

Lieb, Frederick G. "One-Armed Gray Is 'Just Another Player' to Pilot Sewell— and That's Okay with Pete." *The Sporting News*, March 22, 1945, p. 6.

_____. "Gray's Wondering If He's Making Good." *The Sporting News*, June 28, 1945, p. 5.

Mead, William. *Baseball Goes to War*. Washington D.C.: Farragut, 1985.

Miller, Donald L. & Richard E. Sharpless. *The Kingdom of Coal: Work, Enterprise and Ethnic Communities in the Mine Fields*. Philadelphia: University of Pennsylvania, 1985.

Pietrusza, David. *Baseball's Canadian-American League: A History of Its Inception, Franchises, Participants, Locales, Statistics, Demise and Legacy, 1936–1951*. Jefferson, NC: McFarland, 1990.

Rea, Larry. "Gray Recalls Early Days, Glory of Being a Chick." *Memphis Commercial Appeal*, April 16, 1978, p. 12.

Sullivan, Neil J. *The Minors*. New York: St. Martin's, 1990.

Thorn, John & Pete Palmer, editors. *Total Baseball*. New York: Warner, 1989.

Wray, John E. "Pete Makes His First Big League Hit." *St. Louis Post-Dispatch*, April 13, 1945.

_____. "Full Time Work Might Help Pete." *St. Louis Post-Dispatch*, June 29, 1945.

Index